The Quest
for Community

Other books by the same author

Suburbia
Control of the City

The Quest
for Community
Social Aspects of Residential Growth

DAVID C. THORNS
Senior Lecturer in Sociology, University of Auckland

London   George Allen & Unwin Ltd
Ruskin House   Museum Street

First published in 1976

© George Allen & Unwin Ltd 1976

ISBN 0 04 300055 x hardback
ISBN 0 04 300056 8 paperback

Printed in Great Britain at the Alden Press, Oxford

To
Gloria, Karen and Joy

Preface

The search for community has been at the centre of much of our planning and development within the cities of the developed and developing world. It is a fascinating area at the heart of our society. It is to an exploration of this area, through an examination of new residential developments, that this book is directed. The illumination of this search will, I hope, assist all those involved in creating our urban future to be more sensitive to and conscious of the social dimensions of the residential environment. I wish to acknowledge the many helpful comments and criticisms I have had from my former colleagues of the Department of Sociology, University of Exeter, particularly Professor G. D. Mitchell and Mr H. D. Munro. My thanks also to Chrissie for her skill with the typewriter and finally to my wife for her encouragement, support and perceptive comments at many stages during the writing of this work.

D. C. THORNS
University of Auckland, 1974

Contents

Tables

Chapter 1

Introduction

The idea of 'community' is one that has captured the imagination of specialist and layman alike. Amongst these are the utopians, the social reformers, the urban planners and the protest and alternative society groups.[1] The various groups have often avoided defining what they have meant by 'community', preferring to use it as a label to cover their particular attitude to or activities within the urban environment. The term has, however, one unifying theme, that of a cohesive group of people, held together by different things which they share, for example, territory, ideas, work, skills and the study of 'community' has reflected these different bases of cohesion.

The consideration of the spatial components of residential areas has been particularly developed by geographers who have examined the distribution of activities within the city, particularly production and distribution of commodities and, more recently, services, for example transport, social welfare services.[2] The basic method for identification of areas has been to fix nodal points and then divide the territory of the city into tributary areas. This leads to a hierarchical model of the city in which the central business district becomes the node of the highest level system. The work of Christaller[3] did much to initiate this particular approach which has been developed by Losch and Berry, amongst others.[4] The problem with this approach is that the activities of an individual produce different spatial distributors, for example, pattern of work, friendships, club memberships, family ties, may all take place in different geographical areas. This produces severe problems in the identification of communities via mapping as the boundaries of territories become very indistinct.

Territory in another sense has also been at the centre of the ecological[5] and ethological[6] ideas of community. The ecologist sees particular populations as being attracted to certain types of territory forming natural areas and this leads to the belief in the crucial role of environment in determining patterns of social behaviour. For example, ecologists demonstrated that in Chicago in the 1920s juvenile delinquency, vice and poverty were concentrated in areas of physical decay. The ecologists' equation of population and territory was stimulated through biological analogy with plant life within eco-systems. This type of biological model has recently re-emerged with the work of ethologists who derive their theories of human community behaviour from the study of primate animals. Here the stress is once again upon the interrelationship of territory and population activities and the local community, the protection of which by such means as covenants, zoning laws, walls and delinquent gangs, is seen as a reflection of man's biological need for security and the occupation of a known and defined territory.

An alternative basis of cohesion is shared social values which give rise to a distinctive way of life. There are two distinct strands here. The first is the study of the process of urbanisation and its effects upon rural and urban dwellers. This is represented by Tönnies in his work on the transformation from 'community' to 'association' as society became urbanised.[7] The community was identified as a group of people united by common norms of behaviour which had arisen through being together under a common tradition. This was reinforced by residential proximity and work centred in the locality. The emphasis here is on the bonds which hold the group together and these are identified as the group norms. This approach, when extended to look at urban society as it was developing, concentrated on distinguishing styles of life which also exhibited similar norms of behaviour. From this grew up such ideas as the 'urban way of life', the 'suburban way of life', 'ghetto way of life' and the 'working-class community'. In all cases there were identified separate norms of behaviour governing life within particular residential areas within the city. The second group were more concerned with putting forward the notion of the 'ideal' community in which men could live more satisfying lives than within the existing urban environment and their idea of community stressed such things as a small scale of operation, mutual obligation, co-operation through informal means rather than by contracts and often a degree of territorial isolation.

Moving from ideas of community based on group norms to those which attempt to construct a community beginning with the individual leads to the interactionist approach.[8] The idea of community as based upon patterns of interaction arises in part out of the use of a technique for studying individual behaviour, in network analysis. In this, the individual is examined in terms of his interactions with others for each of his major activities, for example family, work, leisure, and then this pattern is extended through the examination of the other members of the original subject's network.

This provides a picture of the extent of interaction between network members and the extent of overlap between networks based upon different criteria, for example family and work. The findings have suggested here that the greatest amount of overlapping of networks occurs in older, long-established residential areas and the least in new ones.[9] Here, if there is a link between a particular set of interactions and a territory, this is seen as a mutual reinforcing process rather than a critical relationship. This approach is, however, primarily a descriptive technique which provides little in the way of an explanation for the continuance of the relationship observed.

Communities also have a planning dimension.[10] Residential areas can be planned or unplanned and if they are planned this can be purely physical planning or it can involve physical and social aspects or it can be an attempt to create a community with common territory and shared social values and aims. This attempt can be made either by external planners or by the participants themselves.

The plan of this book is to explore forms of residential areas to see how far these particular ideas of community are identifiable in each area and how far they have produced varied patterns of life for the residents. The consideration of residential areas will be in four groups. The first will examine local authority housing estates, redevelopment schemes, multi-storey complexes, suburbs and commuter villages. These are ones which have been developed with fairly limited objectives as part of existing city areas consequently linked into the existing urban spatial and social structures. The second will be new towns which mark a break with the existing city and represent a new concept in residential development. The third will be the squatter areas of the developing city which are not part of the planned city structure but rather an expression by the residents themselves in concrete form. The fourth will be the explicitly ideologically based communities of religious and other groups. The final chapter will seek to identify residential components which might point the way to more fruitful developments in community research.

Chapter 2

The Development of New Residential Areas

I DEMOGRAPHIC REVOLUTION

The growth of population in both the more developed and less developed countries has brought with it tremendous pressure upon urban space and resources. The analysis of demographic data shows a number of clear trends. In the more developed countries there is declining rural population, for example in Europe from 170 million in 1970 to an estimated 131 million in 2000.[1] This is coupled with a growing urban population, Europe's rising from 292 million in 1970 to an estimated 438 million by 2000, or 77 per cent of its total population. This same trend is seen in other developed regions such as the United States, Japan, Australia and New Zealand where it is estimated the urban population will rise to 85 per cent of the total by 2000. Within this broad trend there is also the rise of the big cities (over 500,000) which now comprise about 50 per cent of the urban population.[2]

In the less developed countries there is one important difference to the pattern described above. This is the fact that both rural and urban populations are increasing and also that the rural population is and will still by 2000 be larger than the urban population. The United Nations population survey gives the urban population for these regions as 635 million in 1970 and estimates this to rise to 2,155 million by 2000 and rural population as 1,910 million in 1970 and 2,906 million in 2000.[3] The fastest rate of growth will be by urban population which will more than triple by the end of the century. There is also the trend towards large cities with these containing 42 per cent of the urban population.

These demographic changes are the result of three principal factors. These are the rise in the birth rate, the increased survival chances of infants plus the increased life expectancy for adults and the migration of population to the cities from the rural hinterland.[4] There has been discussion and controversy amongst those who have studied the growth of cities regarding the relative importance of these three factors in the growth of cities. Wirth,[5] for example, has argued that if cities relied upon the birth rate and increased life expectancy they would fail to replace themselves because of emigration from the city. He, therefore, argues that migration is a significant factor. This view was no doubt strengthened by the structure of Chicago in the 1920s and 1930s which experienced a series of waves of migrants from both the rural hinterland and from Europe which was one of the factors responsible for the concentric pattern of the city noted by Burgess[6] and incorporated into his concentric zone model of city growth. The importance of the migratory element in the development of the structure of the city is also noted in many of the concepts of the ecological school of urban sociology, particularly those of 'invasion and succession'. In Britain, unlike Chicago, there was less influence from overseas immigration upon the growth of the cities but there was rural–urban migration which, alongside the improvement in health and conditions within the city, which improved the life expectancy of city dwellers, accounted for the rapid growth of the city population in the nineteenth century. Davis,[7] however, in discussing the current patterns of urbanisation, places much less importance upon the role of rural to urban migration and much more on population growth and so implies that cities are reproducing themselves and growing without migration. The population growth of the cities due to improvement in infant and adult mortality is more than enough to sustain the current size of the city. However, migration still occurs and is a factor contributing to the actual growth rates of the city. It is thus difficult to separate entirely these three demographic factors except that currently in many developed countries, because of the high levels of urbanisation, rural–urban migration has ceased to be the main migration characteristic of the city. In Britain, for example, most of the migration is now inter-urban rather than rural–urban. Also in developed countries, the city is now moving into a situation of either stability or population decline. In a stable situation there is replacement, though not necessarily without change in the composition, of the population through migration (inter-urban) and immigration (e.g. Commonwealth into Britain). On the other hand there is population decline when the city population migrate beyond the administrative boundaries of the city.

These changes in the urban population in developed countries have had two main consequences for the development of new residential areas separate from the city. First, new urban residential areas have been created out of rural settlements which have expanded through new housing development, etc. These have been the product of outward migration from the city into planned new towns or expanded existing communities. Secondly, there has been the creation of new peripheral settlements around the city creating the typical suburban development, very often unplanned, around the majority of the cities in the industrial countries and the urban squatter settlements of many developing countries which are products of both rural–urban migration and movement from the city outwards.

The simple analysis of demographic change using figures based on nations as a whole is rather too simple for the analysis of new residential area formation as important changes can be masked within these overall figures. There can, for example, be a redistribution of the population which does not affect the overall proportions of rural and urban. Davis's figures for the United Kingdom show that the urban population has only increased by 1·59 per cent between 1950 and 1970. However, during this twenty-year period there has been a considerable volume of population redistribution with the growth of suburban areas, commuter villages and the new towns; and the associated decline in densities of residence within the city centre areas.[8] It is necessary, therefore, to look beyond these broad demographic trends which give some indication of the scale of urban growth and change to identify some of the factors which have resulted in the evolution of the various types of new residential areas which are observable in the developed and developing countries.

II   ECONOMIC GROWTH AND INDUSTRIALISATION

There have been many explanations for the growth and development of cities, but one of the key factors has nearly always been seen as economic. This is particularly true when the growth of the industrial city is considered. Consequently economic growth has been particularly important in Western experience where the impetus to city growth came in in the nineteenth century following closely the Industrial Revolution and the rise of factory production. The cities grew as employment centres, attracting rural migrant populations who were at the same time being pushed from the land through a decline in agricultural employment brought about by rationalisation within the agricultural sector of the economy. In England and Wales this change was reflected in rapid growth in the total urban population which rose to 72 per cent of the population by 1891. This growth was also reflected in the creation of new urban areas. In 1801 there were 45 urban sanitary areas in England and Wales. This grew to 123 in 1881 and 360 in 1891.[9] Thus the growth in urban population led to the creation of new urban residential areas and the basic reason for this growth was economic development. The nineteenth-century pattern of city growth and urban concentration is reflected in the distribution of basic industries of the United Kingdom, with the cotton industry in Lancashire, the Yorkshire woollen industry and the development of coal mining and iron making. This led to urban growth in the North, Midlands and South Wales, centred in and around the coalfields of Lancashire, Yorkshire, Durham and Northumberland and South Wales. As the twentieth century has progressed and the industrial structure of the country has changed from these industries to secondary and tertiary industries new employment centres have arisen which are located in different regions, for example in the south-east. This has produced population migrations and the development of housing and related pressures upon urban communities in the south, particularly London. This led to the desire to restrict urban growth within the 'conurbations' and develop plans for the devolution of population through enforced limitation and the creation of new residential areas to accommodate the excess city population. This same kind of pattern of economic change has affected to a greater or lesser extent all industrial countries and has led to imbalances within their economies which have resulted in migratory movements and economic disparities between the various regions of the country. To limit the effect of these economic changes most industrial countries have adopted policies of limitation upon urban and industrial growth in some regions and its active promotion by fiscal and other means elsewhere. This has in some cases hinged on the development of new urban residential areas to form the basis for such growth. For example in Japan, the strategy of limiting both the growth of population and concentration of industry upon Tokyo was adopted.[10] This involved setting physical limits to the development of Tokyo and the promotion of a number of new towns to take population from the city and act as centres of new industrial development. In a recent study of strategies adopted in European countries Rodwin[11] has drawn attention to some of the major imbalances of European countries, e.g. between the south-east and other areas of Great Britain (particularly the development areas), in France between Paris and particularly the west and south-west, in Italy between the industrialised north and the agricultural south and in the USSR there have been policies to curb the growth of Moscow and to encourage growth in other less well developed areas of the country, particularly the land beyond the Ural mountains. This development of planning controls and public policy decisions about where and on what scale urban growth should be permitted within a country has obviously limited the role of pure economic forces in the promotion of urban growth and the creation of new residential areas. Therefore, it is necessary to look beyond this to other factors which are now assuming equal or greater importance.

The pattern of urban growth and its relationship to economic development which has just been outlined for the developed industrial countries has been rather different in many of the developing countries. Hoselitz[12] in a penetrating analysis of the role of economic development in Indian cities found significant differences between their pattern of economic growth and that of Western European cities. The growth pattern of Indian cities during the twentieth century he found to have greater similarity with nineteenth-century European cities in terms of their social structure and demographic development than with twentieth-century European cities. Having established that this would be the most meaningful basis for comparison he then goes on to explore in some detail the differences which he found between the Indian and European pattern of growth. One of the significant differences he found related to the role of the city as a source of employment and the type of employment being created. The European city of the nineteenth century had a much higher proportion of its population engaged in manufacturing industry, one-quarter compared to one-tenth; this was coupled with a much smaller agricultural population than found in twentieth-century India, a half, compared with two-thirds. The Indian situation thus presents a rather lower level of industrialisation and this linked with the character of the industrial sector which is composed of small-scale enterprises has had consequences for the employment situation within the city and there are doubts as to the role of the city as an inducer of social change. The economy of India is consequently at a lower level of industrialisation than was characteristic of the Western European countries so urban growth has proceeded with smaller accumulations of industrial capital and fewer industrial employment opportunities for the migrants to the city and for the increasing city population produced by the twentieth-century improvements in health, hygiene, etc. This has meant that while the European cities were characterised for most of the nineteenth century by labour shortage, the Indian cities have been areas of labour surplus and unemployment which has affected all types of employment, i.e. both manual and non-manual. The population of the cities has, therefore, not increased primarily in response to the pull of employment opportunities but more from the push of the rural population. The pressure upon land in the rural areas in India has increased due to overpopulation, this labour surplus necessitating migration. The effect of these twin forces of economic development and rural population pressures has been to create urban growth and the creation of new 'squatter communities' of high density and a low level of amenities. A further factor which has led to the tendency of the cities to be an amalgam of small communities with village-like structure and development is that many of the cities are the product of colonial origins and development, e.g. Bombay, Calcutta and Madras. These consist of an elite which is westernised and oriented to national values and is involved in state and national political activities and the ex-rural migrants who tend to re-create the village within the cities through the caste and familial systems which still operate in private, inter-personal relationships even though at the public activities level the distinctions of caste have been reduced.[13] The economic structure of the city, noted above, of small enterprises, encourages the maintenance of this kind of community structure.

From the work of Hoselitz and others based on examination of the cities of India and South-East Asia[14] it becomes clear that the pattern of growth has been different with economic growth not being a primary variable. In these countries it is the rural land pressures and population densities which have 'pushed' the population from the countryside into the cities. This, together with the slower rate of economic development, has created the conditions observable in many developing cities of unemployment, inadequate housing and slow development of facilities for the increasing population. The increased city population produced by migration and natural causes, has created conditions under which new residential areas are being created and these are very often unplanned and in many cases built by the migrants and city dwellers themselves on land often illegally acquired from either public or private landlords. This process creates the squatter settlements which have become a distinct feature of the developing cities in Asia.[15]

The growth and development of cities in Latin America has also been analysed by urban sociologists to try to discover more about the relationship between economic growth and the creation of new residential areas.[16] Here again, as in the case of India, there appears to be evidence that city growth is a product of rural migration as much if not more so than economic growth. The industrial level of the countries has been found to lag behind the level of urban growth, although there have been differences particularly in the levels of capital formation between India and Latin America, which have led Hoselitz[17] to suggest that Latin American countries represent a middle position between Western development and that found in Asia. However, industrial employment lags considerably behind that of the more highly developed countries and the unemployment rates for the cities are high. Development is, therefore, again characterised by labour surplus rather than labour shortage as in nineteenth-century Europe. Also, as in the Indian city, the structure is one of sharply differentiated social groups which vary from the elite which is again westernised (although in this case it owes its origins to Iberian culture) to the urban poor who still retain many of the characteristics of a 'rural peasant community', as Oscar Lewis[18] found in his study of rural migrants to Mexico City. The most visible effect of this migration to the cities has been the increased levels of unemployment and the congestion and deterioration in many aspects of the city environment. Again on the edges and other vacant areas of land within the city are found new communities of squatter population springing up. These are variously named as *favela* in Brazil, *banda de miseria* in Argentina, *barriada* in Peru and *tugario* in Columbia. The growth rate of this kind of urban population has been about 2·9 per cent per annum in recent years.[19] Once again there can be seen quite clearly the influence of migratory pressures produced by the land pressures and reforms of the rural areas producing new urban areas. A further influence upon the rural migrant is the rising aspirations of the population for a higher standard of living which is identified with urban employment and living.

III   GROWTH OF NEW RESIDENTIAL AREAS IN BRITAIN

(a)   *Structural Features of Society*

Having now examined the question of urban growth in a general context it is valuable to concentrate upon one particular case for a more detailed examination. In Britain there is strong evidence to suggest that city growth was similar to the general pattern put forward for urban growth in Western countries, with cities growing as a response to industrial development. The population was attracted from the land by the growth of employment and by the structural reform of agriculture which created a labour surplus. Here it was this reform rather than population pressure which led to the 'push' of migrants from the countryside to the growing cities. As the twentieth century progressed, however, there has been an increasing amount of intervention by successive governments into the 'pure' economic system. Intervention began in earnest in the 1930s and was the result of two separate nineteenth-century traditions merging. These were the concern with the employment conditions of the working class, e.g. with the hours worked, the regulations regarding the working of women and children and the physical conditions of work.[20] This movement gradually broadened its concern to one with the problems of industrial society, particularly poverty and structural unemployment. The other tradition was the nineteenth-century concern with health, housing and hygiene which led to protests against the living conditions of the poor in many nineteenth-century cities. This group was instrumental in the nineteenth-century public Health Acts which marked the beginnings of the intervention of the Government into the control of the city. As the twentieth century progressed these two strands came together and gradually there emerged a policy for the growth and development of cities and the location of industrial growth. This policy has been broadly accepted by successive governments although the methods chosen to achieve the ends of the policy have varied.[21] This policy has had three principal aims. First was that the growth of the conurbations, particularly London, should be limited in both population and employment. This policy was first fully elaborated in an influential report after the Second World War by Sir Patrick Abercrombie[22] in his plans for London which laid down specific size and boundary limits for that city and proposed that the excess population should be rehoused in overspill and new town developments. The second aim was to promote growth in the regions, particularly the outlying regions of the country and those with declining industries to try to correct the imbalances in employment and population that were being created. This policy has been implemented through a variety of financial incentives in the form of development grants to firms willing to move to the 'development areas' to open new factories. Also in 1965, regional economic development councils were created by the Labour Government to prepare development plans for their particular region in an attempt to produce co-ordinated economic planning and growth in the various regions. The third aim was to change the form of growth in the conurbations.

The policy of control of employment and growth and the refashioning of the growth of the conurbations was set out in the Abercrombie Report on London and the principles behind this have since become widely accepted as those upon which urban growth should be based. The Abercrombie plan covered an area extending some thirty miles from the centre of London and divided the area into four concentric zones within which the principles outlined above were given concrete expression in a series of specific proposals. The inner area of London was at the time of the plan built up at high density and had a deficiency of good housing with modern amenities. The proposals of the plan were that it should be redeveloped in order to improve the housing stock, the road system and create provision for open spaces. These changes would create a surplus of about one million which would have to be rehoused outside the London area. The second ring was that of the inter-war suburbs. These had been developed at low densities and contained a fairly stable population thus little change was required in this region. The third ring was to be the 'green belt' which was designed to contain the growth of London so in this ring there was to be a limitation imposed upon the building of new property. This limit was set initially at 125,000. The final ring was the area beyond the green belt which would take the majority of the surplus population in either new towns (eight planned for the London area in latter part of the 1940s) or in the expansion of the existing towns and villages. In either case these movements of population created new communities or at the very least radically transformed the social and economic structure of the existing areas.

The extension of this Abercrombie thesis of city growth control, green belt, and new towns beyond the green belt has been adapted and applied to the other conurbations of Great Britain. For example, Glasgow has developed new towns at East Kilbride and Cumbernauld as part of a plan to decentralise and limit its population growth. Similar plans have been developed for the Liverpool area; with Runcorn new town south of the Mersey to relieve some of the growth pressure of the conurbation and the plan for a new town in south Lancashire to alleviate the pressure on Manchester and act as a new growth point within the region. It can be seen that in the development of post-1945 new residential areas, one of the most powerful influences has been not economic growth demonstrated by new industrial based areas but the deliberate policy of governments both as to the need for such residential areas and also as to their siting and subsequent economic development.

There have, however, been other pressures for the creation of new residential areas of both planned and unplanned types from within the cities themselves. Two important factors here have been first, urban renewal which often creates population surpluses which have to be rehoused either on the periphery or outside the city, this policy being subject to the availability of land for development. Secondly, urban congestion which leads to the voluntary migration of upper income groups to suburban and rural areas.

Urban renewal nearly always creates surplus population of either a temporary or permanent character, due to a number of factors. First, density requirements have changed since the older areas were built consequently not all the people can be rehoused on the same spot. Secondly, and perhaps more important, are the changes which have taken place in the structure and functions of areas of the city. The cities currently require more space for their central business, shopping and commercial areas, for their road systems and parking areas. All these affect the areas near the centre which are still available for living after urban redevelopment. The changing pattern of transport which has brought greater reliance by individuals upon the car for travelling to work, shopping and leisure activities within the city has increased the pressure on land in the central areas for roads (inner ring roads, etc.) and car parking. All these pressures are likely to increase unless more drastic action than that yet envisaged is taken to restrict the entry or use of cars in the central areas of cities.[23] To provide housing for the displaced urban population the city authorities have generally obtained land outside their existing boundaries in the neighbouring authority areas where they have constructed housing estates. For example, the building of the 'cottage' estate by the London County Council in the 1920s and 1930s in Essex and Surrey and the development of the Wythenshawe area of Cheshire by Manchester Corporation. In both these cases subsequent boundary changes have led to the incorporation of the areas with the city. The growth outward in this way of local authority housing has been matched by the extension of private development into the rural surrounds of the urban areas bringing with it the development on a large scale of suburban and commuter dormitory villages. A number of different types of new residential areas have developed therefore through the process of urban renewal and outward expansion ranging from those which were planned and developed as a whole by local authorities or a new town development corporation to those which have developed in a much more piecemeal pattern being the product of a number of different builders over a longer time period.

The second consideration is that of urban congestion. The flight from the city to the outer areas has been, in part, based upon social ideological consideration as to the nature of the preferred physical and social environment. This ideology is a mixture of anti-urban and social class values which have exerted a considerable influence upon the pattern of outward migration from the city. It has also been based upon the lack of provisions in the older housing which became socially unacceptable to larger proportions of the population with rising economic and social standards. The generation of these rising demands was also influenced strongly by the pressure and work of the social reformers who drew attention to the contemporary conditions and lack of amenities and their harmful consequences upon the health and longevity of the city populations. By 1913 it had become fully accepted that densities should be reduced and that the population should be housed in houses with gardens and open spaces. In the Tudor Walters housing report in 1913 the figure of 12 to an acre was put forward as a desirable one.[24] This foreshadowed the growth of the 'garden suburbs' in the 1920s and 1930s. The figure of 12 to the acre was the one produced by the influential architect and planner Sir Raymond Unwin[25] who worked with Ebenezer Howard on the development of the first two garden cities at Letchworth and Welwyn.

In the various factors that have been identified so far as instrumental in producing new residential areas within Britain and in many of the other developed countries, it can clearly be seen that the final decisions about their growth and development are the consequence of a number of different decisions taken by both individuals and local and central governments. For example, the recent, though now abandoned, plans to develop the London Motorway box system emerged from the resolution of differing pressure groups, the local and central governments who have to finance the scheme and have the problem of traffic growth and congestion to some of the local residents whose houses, shops, businesses would be affected and living conditions worsened by the construction of roads near their houses, motorists who would stand to gain from the improvements and the environmentalists who see the motorways as further threats to the quality of the present environment.[26] The development of any new scheme for the urban environment can consequently be seen as the result of a series of compromises between alternative actions produced out of the conflicting pressures brought upon the governing authority by the various interested parties. The precise outcome is likely to reflect the current power, influence position of the various groups *vis à vis* the governing body. This is clearly seen in the development of new towns policy in both Britain and the United States.

(b)   *Social and Ideological*

Moving from the structural features of societies, i.e. economic system, population growth, urban renewal and congestion to what might be described as the social and ideological, we can find a further set of influences which have operated to determine the nature rather than number of residential areas which have been developed. Some of the background to the generation of these social ideologies has already been considered in discussing the two strands which came together in the planning policies of the inter-war and post-war periods. There are, however, other equally important strands to the generation of the kind of ideologies which stem from a wider concern with the nature of the human environment and the need not merely to improve it through social reform but to re-fashion it by social revolution and reconstruction. The writing of one man, Ebenezer Howard,[27] at the turn of the century has had a profound influence upon thinking about the nature of the urban environment in Britain and in nearly all other countries of the world. Howard is important as he sketched out both the need for and also the kind of new community which should be developed which would combine the rural and urban element of society into a new synthesis which would preserve and enhance the best features of both. The writings of Howard led to the formation of a movement which was called at first the Garden Cities and Planning Association which was committed to actively promoting the idea of garden cities as a solution to the problems of contemporary urban society. This association later became the Town and Country Planning Association and as such has continued to play an influential role in the development of planning policy in Great Britain. It is very largely due to the influence of this particular body that new towns were accepted as an integral part of post-war planning policy. Howard, in his writing, caught the mood of a substantial section of the middle class who desired a new kind of community which would remedy the faults and failings of the nineteenth-century industrial cities.

The desire for a new kind of community which combined rural and urban into an ideal set of conditions and ways of life was not unique to Howard, although his work has been very influential in terms of twentieth-century developments. There were other idealists who had a desire to create total new communities. It is possible to divide these idealists into those who were visionaries and those who were practitioners who initiated new developments. Fellow visionaries with Howard who also developed new conceptions of the environment were people like St Simon, in the late eighteenth and early nineteenth centuries and Le Corbusier, in the early twentieth century, the latter with his vision of the city composed of multi-storey dwellings set in a park. This would for Le Corbusier produce a more concentrated city to reduce the amount of suburban sprawl and preserve the character of the city. Le Corbusier[28] prepared a plan for the centre of Paris based on these ideas which would have rehoused a greater population than that already living in the area in tall blocks set amidst a park-type landscape with lawns, trees, etc. Or more recently there is the American architect/planner Frank Lloyd Wright[29] with his concept of Broadacre city, the very antithesis of Le Corbusier's conception. There was also in the nineteenth century in Britain the practitioners who were committed to the reform of the existing conditions and they pioneered some interesting new communities. Robert Owen (1771–1858) spans in some ways both movements as he was a visionary who made several attempts to put his ideas into practice in trying to found and develop new communities for the working class in which his political philosophy of socialism might find concrete expression. His pioneering developments of model industrial, residential communities were followed during the century by the less ambitious 'model' communities built by industrialists to house their workers in improved physical conditions. The first of these was constructed by a mill owner near Bradford at Saltaire. This was followed by the development of Bournville by the Cadbury family and Port Sunlight by the Lever family. These were less ideological in that they lacked Owen's utopian conception of a new way of life and were more firmly based upon a desire to create healthier conditions for their workers and so are more closely allied to the nineteenth-century social reform movement. Just as political ideologies have stimulated a desire to found new communities as in the case of Robert Owen, so have religious values led to the creation of new religious-based communities. For example, the growth and development of the Mormon communities in North America such as Salt Lake City in which the structure and organisation were based upon religious beliefs and influence.

In the United States many would have identified one of the social ideological supports for the creation of new communities as being the 'American Dream' of rural independent living. This 'Dream' was seen to be attainable in suburban living which incorporated the 'rural' virtues of American past which are given prominence in the intellectual critics of urbanism in America such as Jefferson, Thoreau and Mumford.[30] This 'Dream' which once provided a springboard for suburban values and growth has now according to the 'critics' of suburbia (Mumford, Jacobs, *et al.*[31]) been betrayed by the indistinguishable monotonous suburban sprawl which has been encircling all American cities in the 1950s and 1960s, so that they now contain over 50 per cent of America's population.[32]

Within the development of contemporary urban residential areas one important element which has to be considered is what kinds of desires are found in the different socio-economic groups regarding the nature of their environment. The dominating themes here appear to centre around the long-standing controversy regarding rural as against urban living. This controversy has shifted from seeing rural life as the one which is infinitely the most acceptable. This view is found prominently in the Romantic movement of the eighteenth and nineteenth centuries which arose in part as a protest against the materialism of industrialising societies and the poverty and squalor of much of the urban environment. The desire for the restoration of man's links with nature, typified by the rural ideal is solved by Howard's imaginative garden city. The shifts and changes in this ideology resulted in varying degrees of favourableness being given to the urban, or suburban communities or the new town as solutions to the problem of what constitutes the ideal environment.

Although these currents in intellectual thought were important, particularly when they became channelled into particular policies like the garden city and new towns movement, also of importance were the social aspirations of the population as it grew in wealth. The twentieth century has witnessed a growing demand from all sections, led initially by the middle class but subsequently spread to the working class, for better housing conditions and more amenities like parks and open spaces within the urban environment and in new town and estate development. This changing pattern of aspirations is reflected in the progressive migration of individuals from the central, older housing areas of the city into the newer suburban areas built to lower densities, and beyond these to the rural hinterland of the cities. These outward movements in search of perceived better higher amenity and status housing has created a clash of interests between policy-makers and planners who have been attempting to control the size and growth of the city and individual aspirations. It is important to realise that housing was and still is an important indicator of position in contemporary industrial societies as these are still largely property based. Owner occupation of a house is thus a prized goal of many individuals.

Emerging out of this consideration of the main strands of social ideology regarding the shape of the residential environment and the structure of new communities, it is possible to identify a broad social philosophy which encompasses many of these elements giving them a cohesion. This philosophy has been strongly influential in the post-war housing and planning departments of government and local authorities in Britain. This social philosophy is one which considers that the best kind of community life (i.e. the one which is most satisfactory to the individual) is provided in reasonably small low density residential areas. These communities are to be built of houses of traditional design which would seek to reconstruct through the design and layout employed, the social organisation of the village with its characteristic of 'communal solidarity'. There is found within it an image of the desirable community life which is held up as the ideal for which all participants, i.e. population, planning authorities, local councils, etc., should strive. This ideal is the one which incorporates the principles of 'community development', i.e. one in which people help themselves, meet and reach a common agreement about their community needs; plan with common consent what they are going to do; carry out by their own efforts the major part of the plan on which they have agreed and are assisted by the expert advice and technical help given them by outside agencies with greater resources than themselves.[33]

This philosophy accepts then, the continuing importance of the large cities but seeks to introduce into their renewal and redevelopment a 'local community' which is then seen as one of the fundamental goals of the social and physical planning of the area. For example, the stated policy of one English local authority in this particular area of community planning is 'to encourage social cohesion and pride in local communities and to provide opportunities for people to participate in the formation of policies affecting their community'.[34] Having stated this aim very little further is said as to how this should be accomplished or the rationale behind coming to this particular view of urban development. Thus the development of cities is normally seen in terms of the building of new neighbourhood units which have as a base a certain size of population and set of amenities like schools and shops. Within these neighbourhoods the basic housing unit is the single family dwelling with garden, and it is expected over time that they will develop into 'communities'. Much attention has been given to the question of balance within these neighbourhood units of population by age, social class and stage in the family cycle to try to determine what kind of balance produces the best conditions for the formation of a 'community'.

The social philosophy we have identified extends from this concern with the shape of the urban community to that of the shape of the urban environment in general, so that we find the formulation of control policies, which include green belts around the city, the new towns, town expansion schemes and key settlement policies, to accommodate the surplus urban population in the kind of living units envisaged earlier, i.e. neighbourhood units. Linked with the emergence of this type of social philosophy are the recent demands for what has been called 'social planning'. Broady[35] writing recently of this kind of development within planning likens it to the growth of the human relations school of industrial sociology. In the past he suggests the predominant ideas have been those of 'architectural determinism' in which it has been argued that the physical structures determine social behaviour and that the relationship between these two factors is essentially a one-way relationship on which it is the social behaviour which is the dependent variable. In social planning, however, there is a shift of emphasis from the physical structure to an interest in the social relationships within the environment and to a concern with the citizen's involvement and participation. This is parallel to the shift in the human relations school to a concern with the social relationships and group formations within industry originally amplified by the work of Mayo and others in the

Hawthorne experiments in the 1930s in the United States.

Cherry[36] in a recent book on planning and its social context has attempted to set out the goals of this new form of social planning. The first of these he sees as assisting in the promotion and furtherance of human contact, to promote vitality in a society through community and personal relationships. (This goal is quite clearly related to the kind of social philosophy that has been outlined above.) This goal is to be achieved according to Cherry by assisting in the provision of both means and opportunities for the furtherance of relationships between individuals. This clearly also has echoes of the community centre movement of the 1950s. The second of his goals is the concern with the needs of minority groups and those requiring special attention and provision such as the old, the young, the chronic sick, handicapped people, etc. The third is that of strengthening and co-ordinating the social services by building up channels of communication through community organisations (here he introduces the idea of community workers and development). Fourthly, the concern with the establishment of priorities which would include the criteria upon which decisions should be made. He concludes by saying that 'one of the keynotes of planning is the ultimate concern with community'.[37] The elements of Cherry's conception of social planning have been included here to show how they form an extension of the existing social philosophy of the development of the urban environment and how still at the centre of this is the notion of the importance of developing 'communities'.

The development of a social philosophy of planning and urban development which concentrates upon the formation of communities as the ideal and has increasingly emphasised the importance of social relationships within the environment has now been identified. This has been one of the profound influences upon the pattern of urban development in the post-war period and has consequently had a very definite influence upon the development of new residential areas; the creation of 'communities' has been at the heart of much planning endeavour and the fundamental concern of a substantial proportion of those involved in the planning and development of new housing areas and the construction of new towns.

One further development of this social philosophy which is important is that of the growth in the desire for public participation and the effect this is likely to have on the future development of residential areas. The growth in the pressure for some formal recognition of the necessity for public participation in the planning and development of their urban environment culminated in the institution into the 1968 Town and Country Planning Act of a requirement being placed upon local authorities to engage in public participation during the various stages of the preparation of policy and structure plans. This area of public participation was examined in a report published later which outlined various ways in which the public might be involved in the planning process more fully.[38] This report, however, acknowledges by drawing a distinction between the educated and active minority and the passive inactive majority, a fundamental problem in this whole procedure which is likely to perpetuate some of the problems of alienation from the planning process felt by many working-class people who are unable to participate or who are unaware of the intricacies of the planning process.[39] The creation of a public involvement of this kind draws attention to the multiplicity of interest groups who are involved in the at times complex decision-making processes that determine the shape of the urban environment. There is the possibility of conflict of interests between the professional planners and the lay members of the local planning committee as they may well share different social philosophies and long-term goals, having different reference groups, the planners have a professional one represented by current planning philosophy and practice whereas the politicians will have varied ones depending on their political party and local involvements. There is the possibility of conflict between these groups and the 'public' (however this is defined) which the Skeffington Report makes clear is not a homogeneous mass but a number of separate groups varying in their degree of articulateness and knowledge of the planning process, and in their social class background. Thus the final plan is likely to be the product in many cases of the synthesis of rival and often conflicting pressures rather than the product solely of one group or even one ideology.

(c) *Planning Systems and Planners*

The final concern of this chapter must be with the group who have increasingly become influential in the development of the environment both urban and rural, the professional planner. Town planning in Britain developed out of the nineteenth-century social reform movement's concern with the amelioration of the physical environment so it was very much *town* planning and focused upon physical aspects of the town, drainage, densities, etc. The first act was passed in 1909 which extended the nineteenth-century public health legislation and gave local authorities powers to prepare schemes for the control and development of new housing. This first act was followed by acts in 1919, 1923 and 1934 extending the powers of local authorities to cover almost all types of land. Also in 1935 there was an act passed which was specifically designed to restrict ribbon development along the roads connecting towns, and was therefore the beginning of the policy of the containment of urban growth. The period up to 1939 was essentially a period of preparation for the new system of planning which emerged after the war. The milestones here were the Barlow Commission's Report in 1943[40] and the Report of the New Towns Committee under Lord Reith in 1945.[41] These two reports provided an outline to the type of system of urban control through the formation of a Ministry of Town and Country Planning (established in 1947) and the form of urban development which was to be encouraged in the shape of the new towns, the first eight of these being designated in the late 1940s. This growth briefly noted here of planning legislation brought with it the growth of a new professional group, that of the town planner. So the background and particularly the 'ideology' of this particular group of individuals becomes an important element in the analysis of the forces operating to produce and modify the urban community.

In order to see some of the differences in the development of planning in other countries the system in another country will be briefly examined. One that has a considerable range of differences in both structure and development is that found in the United States. The first and most important difference between the two systems is that the British system has developed as a system of administrative control integrated with local and national government, so it has been used as part of public policy.[42] In the United States, however, this has not been the case. Planning has been of two kinds. First, there has been a legal framework based on state and federal laws and secondly, an advisory aspect which has been the main area of true planning as this has been independent of government. Until 1964, perhaps clearly indicating the essential difference of approach, there was no United States Federal Ministry of housing and planning, although there were federal agencies through which government money was passed to aid cities in carrying out improvements and renewal programmes, and also to finance home ownership.

As in Britain, American city planning[43] found its early impetus to development in the desire to improve the housing conditions of the working class within the city. This pressure for reform came from public health officials and other allied groups and social reformers. Also at about the same time, the turn of the century, there grew up in America the Municipal Art Movement which was dedicated to producing more attractive cities. In order to achieve this goal, there needed to be planning and control. The movement reached perhaps its high point with the baroque plan for the capital devised by Major Pierre Charles L'enfant. The influence of the movement can also be seen in the Urban Parks Movement which attempted to provide amenities and open spaces within the cities. This movement had as some of its champions Olmstead and Vaux who designed Central Park in New York. The system of planning which emerged as the twentieth century has progressed, has developed in two separate ways. This stems from the doctrine of the separation of powers enshrined in the American constitution of the division of responsibility between the law makers and the administrators. The first kind of planning that was adopted was a form of legal control in the introduction of zoning laws from Germany in the early part of the twentieth century. The establishment of these zoning regulations required in each case the passing of a separate law by each state, or city authority. Thus this system of control spread unevenly across the cities and states of America. The zoning regulation gave the city authorities powers to control the use of land and the densities of development. Therefore, the earliest city planning in the United States was essentially a system of allocating land to different areas and controlling the overall shape of the city in a rather piecemeal fashion. However, developing alongside these zoning regulations was the second element in American planning, the planning commission. These were made up of lay commissioners who were drawn from prominent citizens in business, politics, etc., and staffed by professional planners. The role of the commission was to prepare basic 'master' plans for the long-range development of American cities. These plans were not, however, in any way binding on the local city authorities, rather they were advisory in character. One of the earliest of these 'basic' plans for the growth of the American city was the gridiron plan. The position of the commission, particularly in the early days of their existence, was often ambiguous and depended very heavily upon obtaining the favour of the ruling political groups in the city. This created conditions for conflict between the city politicians and the commission and between the commission and other interest groups—that is, business and commercial interests within the city. Also there was often conflict between the lay commissioners and the professional planners over the goals of city development and the means of achieving these. This more open dialogue between the planning commission and the political and other interest groups demonstrates publicly the conflicts and compromises which are reached in plan making; in contrast to the British context where much of the dialogue takes place within the planning department itself.

The planning system then that has developed in America is different in a number of important respects from the British system and these differences have had an effect upon the development of new residential areas in the two countries. The first American new towns appeared in the 1920s and were privately sponsored and unlike the post-war new towns of Britain, were not the product of any kind of broad public policy for the control of urban growth and redistribution of the population or for the systematic development of the depressed regions. The first government-sponsored new towns appeared during the Roosevelt administration in the 1930s as part of his New Deal strategy to revive America from the Depression, specifically part of the Rural Resettlement Administration Programme.[44] In 1935 plans were prepared to construct eight of the new 'greenbelt' towns, in fact only three were built due to a court action in which a right-wing group, opposed to new towns, defeated the government and also to a shortage of finance. In the 1930s, therefore, the creation of new towns was seen as a means of stimulating economic activity and also the idea of using planning in the wider role as a creative agent extended the perspective of city planning to one of regional planning in which devolution schemes could be seen as an important element.

As the twentieth century has developed American city planning has become characterised by two particular perspectives. The first arguing that stronger government action should be taken to remedy the existing defects of the city structure and create in its place one more capable and responsive to the contemporary social and economic needs of the population. This particular perspective it is claimed has led to an over-emphasis in America on city planning and urban renewal schemes for central city areas and an almost total absence of planning, apart from zoning regulations and sometimes there have not been even many of these, upon suburban growth. The suburb is fast becoming the home of the majority of American white population, leaving the central city areas to become, where they have not already, ghetto areas of coloured population. The other perspective, which has been more common among 'academic planners' in planning schools than amongst practitioners, has been the desire to re-examine the basic ideas and assumptions upon which the American system of planning rests, particularly the separation of the various activities and the relationship of zoning laws, the planning commission and the concentration upon the city and urban renewal.

The first of these perspectives led to the increasing demand for the creation of a federal department of housing and urban development with a political head of cabinet rank. This would bring the whole notion of planning on to a much firmer relationship with the administrative structure of state and federal government. The desire was finally realised in the 1964 creation of a department of housing and urban development. As part of a new look at the urban scene the

Johnson administration proposed in 1965 a new towns programme. The new towns envisaged here were to have all the available public services, and a sufficient industrial and commercial base to provide jobs within the towns for the inhabitants and adequate housing and cultural and recreational facilities for moderate and low income families, as well as the wealthier sections of the society. This programme was, however, never implemented due to the opposition of the mayors and council men of the large cities forming an alliance of opposition to the plans with insurance companies and private developers. This combination of forces was quite sufficient to defeat the attempts by the President to obtain financial assistance for the planning and development of new towns. This failure in government initiative which was blocked by interest groups opposed to public-sponsored new towns has meant that the construction and planning of new towns has been left in the hands of private developers. The role of government has been that of encouragement rather than that of an innovator in this particular field. Again this is a contrast to the British case where the initiative came through government action although the first attempts at new town construction were by private enterprise through the selling of shares in the development company. The increase in the involvement of the federal government in the planning process is one which has gradually grown over time as larger and larger amounts of federal money have been allocated to the cities for urban renewal and similar work. Also the history of American planning and the role of the federal government illustrate the way in which conflict and strains do arise in the system which have a marked influence upon the shape of the environment. It was because of the conflict of interests for example between the city authorities who were anxious to avoid further migrations of their white population to the new towns, and the federal government allied to the conflict between the government policy and the property interests in American society represented by the insurance companies and the private developers that the creation of new towns has stayed in private hands. Also it is this same conflict of interests between the city authorities and their preoccupation with their internal problems and the concentration of resources upon these, allied to the property interests of the private developers and their resistance to planning that has led to the almost total lack of effective planning of large areas of suburban growth around American cities. This has produced often formless, inadequately served residential areas which perhaps symbolise clearly one of the failures of American planning.

Recent change in American planning is again one which has emerged in British planning, an interest in and concern with the idea of social community planning which in part is the outcome of the second perspective noted above, of the total reappraisal of the role and ends of planning.[45] This new concept of community planning differs in a number of ways from the conventional idea of city planning. First, it is concerned with all aspects of the city, its social, economic and physical development. Too often, it is claimed, in the past city planning has concentrated on the latter aspect to the exclusion of all else. Secondly, it encompasses all the programmes and policies developed by the local government which affect in any way at all the economic, social or physical renewal of the city. The last element is that this form of planning recognises the importance of establishing community-wide programmes as part of the process of city government. The idea of a more integrated approach to problems and the direction of development towards certain goals and conceptions of the ideal or desirable environment become important elements in this kind of approach.

The American system of city planning therefore has considerable differences from the one outlined earlier for Britain. The system of planning as it has arisen has had a considerable influence upon the structure and growth of new residential areas within the United States. The differences in the systems of planning have led to reduced amounts of control being exercised in the United States over the form of the entire environment, i.e. urban, rural and suburban. Also the structure of American planning as advisory in the main rather than compulsory as part of the administrative machinery of national and local government has resulted in a much greater variation between cities and states in the policies they have pursued and the range of controls they have practised. Also the structure allows a clearer view of the various groups who have exerted a powerful influence upon the shape of the urban environment and whose conflicting interests have had to be resolved in changes in the city and suburban areas.

The ideologies and role of the planner both as seen by society and the planners themselves are important to the operation of both American and British planning systems. When this question is considered it is clear that there is currently evidence of multiple roles and even identity crises amongst planners searching for new forms of legitimacy.[46] The earliest role of the planner was seen as that of the expert, where the planner derived his authority from his technical skills. This is where planning is seen as a rational scientific activity designed to produce order, efficiency and aesthetic beauty within the city which is seen as disordered. The growth of this idea of the planners' role arises out of the origins of planning already discussed in the reform movement of the nineteenth century. This led to the 'facility planning' of America[47] and the 'amenity planning'[48] of Britain, which believed that through improvements in the physical environment such as parks, playgrounds, community centres, better housing, the problems of the city such as crime, vice, family breakdowns would be solved. The failure of these physical renewal policies to produce changes in social behaviour have led to the idea of human renewal through education, social casework and community development to be linked with physical renewal. An example of this philosophy can be seen in the 1965 Model Cities programme in the United States. A second role is that of the planner as a public employee deriving his authority from the politician and operating within an administrative framework, as in Britain. Here the planner translated the objectives laid down by politicians into land-use patterns. This activity places the planner in a situation of potential conflict where he is both judge and advocate of particular policies. These two traditional roles of the planner both have as their main concern the physical environment and have led to the dominance within the profession of engineers and architects and the emphasis within planning education upon the physical sciences and the legislative framework of planning.

Dissatisfaction with these roles has increased in recent years and found expression in a number of new developments. The first of these is known as advocacy planning.[49] The planner here has moved to work with the planned for, often leaving the planning agencies and drawing up alternatives to the master plan strategy for the urban area. This new role involves a change to an emphasis upon a consumer orientation and the much greater involvement of the public in the planning process. This movement towards advocacy planning has been stimulated by the emergence of urban protest groups, like tenants' protection societies and the race riots in the ghettos of American cities in the 1960s. A further factor has been the entry of social scientists into planning agencies and departments. The final area of change has been the recognition by some planners that urban planning is a value-laden activity. Therefore, their explicit concern is with the implementation of particular social values they themselves believe in, such as the desire to produce an egalitarian society through the reduction of racial and economic inequality. This approach has tended to split planners into conservatives and progressives, the former holding to the traditional role of physical planning expert and the latter stressing the primacy of social and economic planning. This more radical stance has brought planners in America and Britain into open conflict with planning commissions and local planning authorities.[50] In America this has centred on the continuation by the commissions of the production of master plans, a concept seen by the progressives as no longer valid within a consumer oriented type of planning in which there must be a variety of possible plans rather than just one.[51]

In this chapter there has been an attempt to isolate some of the processes which have been important in the development of new residential areas in both developed and developing countries. In some cases these new areas have been carefully planned and built as part of a national policy of planned decentralisation or stimulation of depressed regions; in others they have grown up in a much more haphazard and unplanned way. The chief influences which have been identified at the structural level are demographic, economic, urban renewal and congestion. Also of importance has been the development of social philosophies and ideologies which have strongly supported the idea of creating 'communities' as the only truly satisfying mode of living. Influential here upon the development of this idea in practice has been the growth of urban planning and creation of a professional group of planners with a particular sort of ideology which incorporates in many cases the belief that the environment could be developed via planning to achieve the goals of the social groups with the most influence upon the formation of public policies.

Having isolated the underlying factors which appear to have influenced the creation of new residential areas it is now necessary in subsequent chapters to examine some of the different types of area which have been produced and thus we shall be able to identify the characteristics associated with each type of environment.

Chapter 3

New Residential Areas

In the previous chapter it has been clear that the notion of 'community' has often been one which has had strong 'utopian' or 'ideal' overtones. 'Community' in this guise has been set up as the ideal towards which social, economic and physical planning should be aiming in the development of new residential areas of all types. But how far have these ideals in fact been translated into practice? Have residential areas which have been designed to develop as communities in fact shown the attributes of the utopian or ideal model? If they have not, why has this occurred? It is due to differing perceptions as to the ideal environment among the various participating groups in the creation of new communities, i.e. architects and planners, developers, local authorities, prospective and actual residents? In this chapter a whole variety of types of new development within the United Kingdom and in other European and American cities will be examined to see how far programmes have resulted in the achievement of the ideals and how far the results in terms of physical and social structure have points of similarity in this variety of settings.

I   LOCAL AUTHORITY HOUSING ESTATES

The first kind of development to be examined is one that has been the most extensively studied in the United Kingdom, that of the local authority housing estates. The development of planning and housing legislation from the end of the nineteenth century onwards increasingly involved local authorities in the control of building and in the provision of housing itself. This housing was directed towards providing for the poorer sections of the community and to providing housing for the rapidly rising population. The further aims of redevelopment and the reduction of congestion and overcrowding have led to a steady expansion of local authority housing provision. The development of housing estates became prominent in the 1920s particularly in the London area which already had at this time a problem of finding land for housing within the administrative boundaries of the London County Council. The London County Council therefore bought land outside its boundaries and developed what have been termed 'cottage estates' during the 1920s and into the early 1930s. The late 1930s saw a decline in this kind of provision due to changes in the financing of local authority house building by the central government. So the 1930s saw much more emphasis upon the development of private suburban estates with money made available through the increasingly wealthy and numerous building societies.[1] After the war however, the local authorities became, and still are, a major developer of housing, particularly for the less wealthy sections of the population. Today local authorities are the most important landlord in the country with 30 per cent of the population having a local authority for a landlord. This compares with 15 per cent of the population who are in private rented property. Much of the property in this latter group is of poor quality in declining areas and the ultimate fate of much of it will be urban renewal and the addition of many tenants to the local authority lists.

The local authority housing estates, built during the 1920s and early 1930s, because of their size and newness, attracted a considerable amount of comment and criticism. According to some observers they were poorly designed and monotonous and lacked the necessary amenities such as work in the area, shopping facilities and community provisions such as a centre for activities, to allow them to develop into viable communities in their own right. Illustrative of this early type of estate is the London County Council development in Essex at Becontree, which was designed to house 120,000 people.[2] The estate was almost entirely residential and the majority in the early years were daily commuters to London for their work. This was changed somewhat by the development of the Ford company in Dagenham and other industry in the neighbouring areas during the 1930s. Arising out of the dissatisfaction with the planning of these estates was the concern during the immediate post-war period among urban sociologists to study the development of areas of new housing to assess their effect upon traditional patterns of behaviour. The focus of these studies was upon the influence of the physical structure of the environment, i.e. whether the estate was planned in culs-de-sac, straight roads, squares, terraces, etc., upon the development of social relationships, and the presence or absence of a sense of and spirit of 'community'.[3] This latter was seen as related to social provision in the form of community centres. Underlying these interests was the desire to answer the broader question of the social changes which occur within the community and to a family through relocation.

From these studies conducted in the 1950s in such places as Liverpool, Sheffield,[4] Oxford[5] and London,[6] it is possible to build up a fairly good picture of the characteristics of the residents and the structure of their 'way of life' in these new local authority housing estates. The residents were, in the first place, all tenants of particular local authorities and had been able to exercise little or no choice as to where they would like to live. They had either been compulsorily rehoused as part of a slum clearance and redevelopment scheme or else they had moved to the top of the housing list. The social composition therefore of the estates was and still is almost entirely working-class manual workers. The concept of 'neighbourhood' which is often associated with the planning of these estates has come, because of this, to be virtually synonymous with working-class housing in the United Kingdom.[7] The fact that the occupants are from the lower income classes means that movement to the new housing areas has often been associated with financial problems or strains due to the increased costs of travel to work, and travel to visit relatives still living either in the older area or living in different new housing areas. The rent levels are also likely to increase on moving to a new local authority dwelling due to the higher level of amenities. The residents of the new estates come mainly from the older central areas of the city which have had a high proportion of relatives and parents living together within a comparatively small area. This has meant that the new resident has to leave behind the system of kinship support which had in the past been an important element in the stability of the older working areas in the centre of cities. The change, then, to the new estate produces a reduction in the frequency of contacts between the individual and his parents and other relatives and thus leads to the development of a home-centred way of life rather than one which appears more 'community centred' or perhaps more accurately described as kinship centred. The estates were characterised because of this 'home-centredness' by few clubs and generally low levels of social participation in organised social activity of this type. Also noted in this respect was, on the whole, a lack of leadership for voluntary association activity. The favoured forms of social activity were in public, essentially anonymous ones, e.g. the cinema. On specific kinds of social activity sometimes cited as being ones which are affected by rehousing, religious behaviour and political allegiance, there is not a great deal of direct evidence. What there is suggests that religious activity in terms of attendance at churches shows some decline and political behaviour would appear to be unchanged. This changed pattern of family activity gives rise to the new housing estate being seen as an unfriendly place with low levels of neighbouring and in general a suspicion of neighbours as they are an unknown quantity. The studies here suggest that people, on the whole, try to guard against uncertainty and this means not initiating new relationships with people who live in close proximity but with whom the person has had no previous contact.

The reduction in family and kinship contacts together with the lack of social participation in organised activities in clubs and societies within the new housing estates suggests that the residents are unwilling to play new and unfamiliar social roles. This unwillingness to establish these kinds of relationship means that increasingly the assessment of neighbours will be based upon external criteria of their homes, gardens and other possessions. This emphasis upon what would then become status symbols for allocation and placement within the estate would then facilitate the rise of status competition, with its subtle but determined pressures upon the residents towards acquiring the symbols of status or engaging in status-giving activities.

There are two wider perspectives which have been consistently explored in studies of new estates of this type. These are the status distinctions within the working-class inhabitants and the division of activities into the 'public' and 'private' spheres in a developmental way as the life of the estate forms over time.

The status divisions within the housing estates have centred around the division into the 'roughs' and 'respectable'. This division occurs in many of the studies and lies between the small family, higher status, possibly more upwardly mobile 'respectable group' and the lower status, large family, social problem 'rough group'. The relationships between these two groups have often determined whether the community centre activities continue after the initial period as a unified activity or separate out into one dominated by one of these groups. In a study of a Liverpool estate, for example, it was the 'rough' group who dominated the activities of the community centre and the 'respectable' group which withdrew from this kind of corporate activity. In a study of Watling[8] the position was reversed.

The second perspective is the one which has sought to establish if the pattern of social relationships and organisation particularly regarding the 'public social life' of the estate follows any particular pattern which can be identified in each case. This examination has led to the development of what has been termed the 'phase' hypothesis of community development.[9] This hypothesis suggests that there are three phases to activities on new housing estates and they are marked by varying degrees of 'public' social activity. The first phase covers the first three to six months or so of the estate's life. This is the period during which the roads are unmade or in process of being laid, gardens are bare and frequently unfenced and the individuality which appears later is not yet stamped upon the houses. The characteristics of exploration and openness are the main features of social relationships with a considerable amount of friendliness between neighbours, and sharing of equipment and news, the latter, particularly about the estate, the progress or otherwise of the laying of the roads and completion of outstanding building work quickly producing a ready audience. The feature of this high level of the social relations and interaction is the sharing of common problems which produces this favourable attitude towards neighbours. This structuring of relationship leads to the easy formation of groupings at the total estate or neighbourhood level, the formation of residents' associations to more forcefully argue the case of the new residents with the developers and the local authority. The initial phase gives way to the second phase when the estate is beginning to 'settle down'. It is no longer possible to know all the residents and the continued growth of the housing estate begins to threaten the intimacy built up in the first phase between neighbours and other estate dwellers. The new residents are more difficult to incorporate into the existing group structures as the original unifying forces in the shape of common problems is now receding, thus the groups begin to weaken their bonds and to disintegrate. Also there occurs now the formation and stabilisation of internal status differences within the voluntary associations, i.e. community centre organisation or residents' associations, etc., and also within the physical sub-units of the estate. These changes are reflected in a decline in enthusiasm and support for organisations representing 'community interests'. This phase again over time gives way to a third phase during which the estate breaks down into smaller social groupings based upon newly established patterns of friendship and neighbouring. This phase also can lead to the relative isolation of individuals and families on the estate who are not part of any organisation.

II   URBAN RENEWAL

In America, unlike the United Kingdom, the emphasis in the urban renewal programme has been upon private enterprise assisted by federal grants and loans. The urban renewal was initiated in the Housing Act of 1937 and since then appears to have acquired three aims.[10] The first was the goal of a 'decent home and a suitable environment' for every American family. This was seen as the task of replacing the slums with standard housing with modern amenities. Secondly was the redevelopment of the central city areas, particularly the central business districts. Thirdly, out of a dissatisfaction with piecemeal unco-ordinated development, has grown up the goal of the planned city based upon a community renewal programme. This latter goal is reflected in the requirement of the federal government in 1954 that localities must have a 'workable programme for community improvement' before they could receive urban renewal assistance. Again unlike the United Kingdom, the problems of engaging in urban renewal have often arisen from the necessity for each authority to seek legislative and administrative approval for the schemes, due to the separation of powers in planning between the courts and local authorities. This has meant that the schemes have been 'exposed to the conflict of internal and external interests, to competing jurisdictions, competing sub-bureaucracies, and an endless array of interested private groups. Any one of a *combination* of these may develop the power to revise, delay, obfuscate, or forbid action'.[11] This clearly demonstrates the way in which the urban renewal programme and therefore the community structures which emerge do so out of the resolution of conflicts at all levels in the political and administrative systems.

In a recent United States Housing and Home Finance Agency Report on relocated families[12] it is possible to compile some perspective on the characteristics and patterns which are likely to emerge in these new areas which are the product of this form of urban renewal. The families involved in the renewal programme were all of low income and the incomes were lowest amongst the non-white population which was rehoused. The majority of the people involved (70 per cent) relocated themselves but of these the majority had some assistance from public agencies (90 per cent). Home ownership was found to increase from 33 to 37 per cent although the majority were still tenants. The composition of the renewal families showed a slight majority of non-white families (53 as against 47 per cent), with the median size being the three-person household. The families had been at their previous house for more than five years and had been, on the whole, well established with well structured social relationships. This is illustrated by the study of Gans of the urban villagers, a group of Italianites in Boston threatened by urban renewal. Gans found the West End to be a socially cohesive society in which peer groups and kinship structures provided valuable integrative functions.[13]

The effects of urban renewal are also hinted at in this report where they suggest that the social impact of rehousing can be seen in the loss of familiar places and neighbourhoods which may lead to a degree of social isolation for the rehoused family. Also the rehousing brought longer journeys to work for 37 per cent and shorter for 13 per cent which is a fairly large rise in the commuting element although the report does not indicate the time that commuting involves. There were also rent increases for the rehoused families to face. These were greatest amongst the families who relocated themselves. On average the increase was of the order of 3 per cent in the median proportion of their income taken up by their rent. The majority were rehoused in single family dwellings with the balance moving into apartment houses.

The report concentrates upon the physical and economic changes which occur and says little about the effects upon social relationships and the kind of 'community' which is or is not created. The hints that there are on this suggest a decrease in 'communal' relationships at least in the initial period of the renewal programme.

The United States pattern of development thus provides points of similarity and contrasts with that of the United Kingdom. The greater importance of the private market gives at one level greater choice in the United States but at another it emphasises the disparities of income and socio-economic status, with public housing being occupied by elderly white residents or Negro, Puerto Rican, etc., families.[14]

Having now examined the United Kingdom and United States, it is valuable to examine a society in which the housing market has not been operated on the free market principle and where the economy of the society and its housing policy has been centrally planned. In Czechoslovakia there is a low degree of urbanisation with the majority of the population living in communities of less than 2,000 population, and only five cities of 100,000 and only one, Prague the capital, of over 500,000. The slow growth of cities has meant that urban renewal is concentrated in a small number of cities and does not present the same kind of problem as it does in many European countries. The housing system is a mixed one, so there are many different types of housing existing side by side, e.g. private ownership, co-operatives, business-controlled and state enterprise. However, rents for property are subsidised as housing is considered in part as a social service, thus rents are a small proportion of the families' budget. As the rent level does not, as in a free market economy, determine choice there is not the usual relationship between level of income and quality of dwelling found in most West European and American cities. This means that there is not a concentration of the poorest individuals in the worst housing in the dilapidated centres of the cities.[15] Also there is no rent differential between the centre and the suburb, therefore choice of residence is decided upon criteria other than financial. The housing allocation policy in respect to new property was guided by criteria of need both for key employees in local business and in terms of size of family. Both these have favoured younger families, consequently there is some correlation to be found between the age of the house and the age of the occupant.

Turning now to the question of urban renewal areas and their development, Musil,[16] on the basis of the available data, presents three categories of redevelopment areas:

1 Slums with imminent need for reconstruction for both social and hygiene reasons; standard of housing low; buildings in a critical condition.
2 Areas with low housing standard but no social pathology, elderly inhabitants with low incomes near the city centre.
3 Housing estates formed of old tenements with a low standard of technical equipment.

Having outlined these three categories Musil goes on to state that nearly all Czechoslovakian redevelopments are concerned with areas falling into the second category.

The studies that have been conducted have looked at the structure of the redevelopment areas rather than the results of movement. The bulk of the residents are older citizens with 40 per cent actually retired. This age structure means that they have moved through and out of the family building cycle and are now mostly two-person families. They have also now low average incomes and low rates of social mobility. The social structure of the clearance areas is marked by the continued importance of the 'modified large family'. This is a modified country family system which has been adapted to the urban society. The existence of this system in these areas is shown by the presence of a large number of mutually related people, existence of mutual help among these relatives living in close proximity, including financial help, household help, and assistance with looking after the children and finally by the existence of social contacts and visiting between those relatives as the most important set of social relationships of the families. In the survey of four city centre areas it was found that the total number of relatives living nearby was between 50 and 67 per cent whereas for a new housing estate in Prague the proportion was only 27 per cent. This clearly suggests that the modified family structure is likely to be affected by rehousing bringing about a reduction in the frequency and strength of kinship relationships. The importance of relatives is further demonstrated by the examination of leisure in which the families were asked what they had done the previous Sunday. The majority answered that they had visited relatives. One important difference found in this study was that unlike in British data the likelihood of relatives living together was greater in the higher income and occupational groups. The people in the redevelopment areas therefore were strongly family centred in the wider sense of kinship involvement, not in the narrow sense of nuclear unit involvement. This was also reflected in the limited significance attached by those studied to neighbour relations.

Gaining some further insight into the effects of the redevelopment upon the residents of the development areas is data obtained in the study concerning the residents' preference for house types and areas. The majority (78–79 per cent) either wished to remain in the same place or in the same district. In terms of type of dwelling preferred, the most desirable was seen as the well-equipped flat with 46–49 per cent of the respondents citing this. Two-storey houses were only preferred by 14 and 29 per cent. This illustrates another interesting contrast with the data for Britain regarding preferences for flats as against conventional two-storey semi-detached housing.

The data for Czechoslovakia presented here does then show a number of interesting variations in the pattern of settlement within the city and the composition of the groups who have and are experiencing redevelopment. The effects and structure of the new areas suggested in these studies, however, does point towards the trend already noticed of decreasing familial contacts and thus the possibility that the new areas will be ones in which people experience greater social isolation.

III   MULTI-STOREY DWELLINGS

(a)   *High Flats*

This form of residential area has mushroomed in the major cities of the world, both in developed and in developing countries since the 1950s. They have grown for a number of reasons. In the first place there has been the developments in building technology which have made their construction possible and solved the problems such as fire control which previously limited their growth. The second has been the intense housing pressures upon the cities faced with large-scale urban renewal and accommodation of migrant populations. This need could be met quickly through the construction of high rise blocks, which were also thought to be cheaper as they saved on architects' costs, the building was prefabricated, etc. The third factor was they could be sited close to the centre as part of urban renewal and would be able to rehouse the old, densely packed population at higher densities than conventional housing. This proximity to the centre would also reduce commuting to work and also help the residents retain their old links with the centre and central areas. Finally it was considered they would help to conserve land by providing higher density development both within the city and also on the periphery where land was becoming increasingly difficult for local authorities to obtain.[17] These various factors led to a rapid growth of this form of new development in the 1950s and 1960s.

The growth of high rise flats was throughout Western and Eastern Europe as can be seen by development around, for example, Stockholm, Amsterdam where the new area of Bulmermeen[18] will provide 92 per cent of its houses in blocks of 9–10 storeys, Zurich, London and most other major British cities, Moscow and Prague. Outside of Europe there has been development in many cities, those which have been studied include Hong Kong[19] and Melbourne.[20] In Britain, for example, local authorities had built around 300,000 flats in high rise buildings by 1968–9 and had a further 79,000 under construction.[21] The heights of these flats have varied rising to over 21 storeys in Glasgow and in a recent plan for Hong Kong a block of over 50 storeys has been proposed. There has in the late 1960s been a move away from high blocks towards medium-sized and more varied mixtures of flats and terraced housing. This in Britain has been partly the result of changes in government subsidies for local authorities which have removed the financial incentive for building high and partly because of public disquiet sparked off by such things as the Ronan Point collapse. One point of contrast between Britain and many other of the European countries has been the predominance of local authority construction for low income groups whereas in many of the European cases the development has been privately sponsored by a variety of groups, such as housing associations, giving rise to much greater diversity of design and facilities.

Studies of this type of development from Britain, the Netherlands and Melbourne have enabled a picture to be built up of the physical and social aspects of life in these areas. In terms of physical structures they appear to be reasonably satisfactory in that they provide a much higher level of amenities, and are better designed than the housing of the older clearance areas. Problems of the design centred around lifts, staircases, and lack of ability to alter the physical arrangements or have a garden which could fulfil a similar need of self-expression and establishment of identity. The majority of flat dwellers did not see it as an ideal physical environment and in one survey 60 per cent expressed their desire to move to a conventional house with a garden.[22]

The social aspects of flat life centre around their effects upon family life and social isolation. Family life is particularly affected where there are small children under five. Because of the situation, both child and mother tend to become housebound.[23] The difficulties do not end once the child becomes older as there still remain the problems of supervision of outside play and the rather unimaginative surroundings for the child to grow up in. Here the Melbourne[24] study which examined both high rise and four-storey blocks found that the latter were much more satisfactory from the point of view of children's play. The second aspect, that of social isolation, is particularly seen in the young mothers, single-person households and the elderly. In the Melbourne study, for example, it was found that, in the high rise, under 50 per cent of the occupants had friends on the estate whereas in the four-storey units without lifts 75 per cent of residents had friendships on the estate. The isolation of families arises through the excessively self-contained nature of the high rise flat in which there is no opening on to the outside world at a point where everyday activity takes place, the windows for example look out high above the world. This lack of contact points, like gardens, streets, provides no easy means for the establishment of neighbour and friendship relations.[25] These characteristics of high rise blocks have led some investigators to the view that they only really suit those who are self-sufficient and can cope with a 'methodical and self-contained existence'.[26] It is further suggested that these are found in the middle and higher income groups, not the low income groups who inhabit the high rise flats at present. High rise flats of the local authorities also are seen to lend themselves to paternalism which limits the exercise of initiative and responsibility by the tenants.

One further area of research which has raised a number of questions about this type of development is that regarding the relationship between urban crowding, population density and various forms of stress both physical and mental. This research at present shows rather contradictory findings with, for example, recent work of Marmor[27] producing what he calls 'strongly suggestive evidence' that overcrowding may well be a significant source of emotional stress. He also points to the increase in psychosomatic disorders such as coronary thrombosis and hypertension, as densities, measured by population per acre, are increased. However, in other recent studies somewhat different findings are presented, for example Mitchell[28] in his study of Hong Kong, where he claims that densities 'do not affect deeper and more basic levels of emotional strain and hostility'. In a further recent study in New Zealand[29] it was found that psychological but not physical disorders were positively related to density.

The combined evidence of physical and social analyses of high flat development have shown that they fail to provide the easy solution to the housing problem that they were originally thought to be in the 1950s. They have turned out to be expensive to build, maintain and service, they do not save land if they are built with proper regard to amenities and they tend to dominate the environment in a way that changes the architecural balance of the area.[30] The social aspects also show that they only suit a small number and many feel relatively deprived and look to the time when they can move into a conventional house. The population, therefore, is likely to be unstable which will not readily form into communal groups and the ideals and values for which they seek are external to their residential environment.

(b)   *Other Forms of Multi-storey Development*

In France *les grandes ensembles*, which are large-scale developments of multi-storey complexes, of moderate height, are a good example to consider.[31] The growth of these areas was a response to the post-1945 housing shortage in France. The developments have been the product of both public and semi-public bodies but have had in the majority of cases a measure of public finance. The largest group, 58 per cent, have been dependent for their finance upon 'Les offices publics d'HLM.' This organisation has been responsible for an even higher proportion of 'grandes ensembles' built in the provinces (4 out of 5). This pattern of development has resulted in virtually all the apartments being for rent rather than owner-occupation, with only 5 per cent owner-occupation being found in *les grandes ensembles* compared to 42 per cent in France as a whole. The distribution of the development of this kind of new urban development has been split almost equally between the cities of the provinces and the Paris area where nearly half of all *les grandes ensembles* of France are built.

From an extensive study of *les grandes ensembles* by P. Clerc *et al.*[32] in 1965 it is possible to examine the chief characteristics of these areas and assess the extent to which they constitute new community structures. This study examined 190 *grandes ensembles* of which 91 were taken from provincial cities and the rest from the Paris area. The dwellings of which these areas were constructed ranged from three- to more than seven-storey buildings with 97 per cent of the building falling into this range. This compares with only 24 per cent of the housing of France as a whole. Therefore, from the physical structure viewpoint these areas do constitute a new type of urban development. Clerc's study looked at the demographic and social structure of *les grandes ensembles* and at aspects of the satisfaction of way of life of the inhabitants.

From their analysis of the demographic structure, Clerc and his colleagues are able to show that these areas differ from France as a whole in a number of respects. They have a larger than average household size (4·10 persons compared to 3·11 persons); they have younger heads of households, with the majority below 45 (77:37 per cent) and higher proportion of married people (88 per cent). This means that these areas are predominantly ones of young married people with children (77 per cent of households have at least one child) of school age or below.

The social structure similarly shows some variations from that of France as a whole and also between *les grandes ensembles* of Paris and of the provinces. On the whole these areas show higher proportions of non-manual workers than are found in the rest of the population with the exception of owners of businesses. These are quite markedly under-represented in both the Paris and provincial *grandes ensembles*. The other important difference is the very small number of non-active members of the work force as heads of households, only 7 per cent compared with 29 per cent for France as a whole. This is a reflection of the age structure, there being very few older retired people living in these areas. This leads to the areas having a higher than average income level.

The levels of satisfaction and the things people cited as advantages give some indication of the way of life desired by those moving to these new areas. Overall they found 54 per cent of the population to be satisfied with the area, 35 per cent found it acceptable and 12 per cent found it inadequate so were dissatisfied. This figure of 12 per cent was found to be higher than that for other new areas of development (8 per cent). The advantages of *les grandes ensembles* given most often were the situation on the urban fringe which meant cleaner air and easy access to the country (23 per cent) and the apartment itself (23 per cent) with its modern amenities (e.g. 82 per cent had central heating compared with only 20 per cent of all dwellings in France as a whole). The disadvantages of *les grandes ensembles* were seen as distance from the centre of the city (22 per cent), the noise level in the apartment blocks (12 per cent) and the dislike of the neighbourhood as a whole (11 per cent). The origins of those moving to these housing areas is also important with 85 per cent coming from the urban areas on whose periphery are the new developments.

The main characteristics of the population have together with the similarity of physical design given to the areas a high degree of homogeneity. These areas were built primarily as housing developments and thus contain relatively few amenities and community facilities or employment. This means that the majority, 80 per cent in the case of the Paris ensembles and 55 per cent in the case of the provincial areas, have to commute to work. This leads to long working days including up to 160 minutes travel time for those of the Paris 'ensembles' who work in the centre of the city. In the Parisian 'ensembles' there is a certain amount of development of secondary centres of shopping and other commercial provision but this is not as well developed in the provincial suburban areas due to their shorter distance from the central areas. This lack of facilities and the long working day do provide problems for the families living in these areas.

Despite the relatively high levels of satisfaction expressed by the residents, this kind of development has attracted a considerable volume of critical comment. This criticism is based on two particular features, both of importance to the consideration of community emergence. These are the quality of the architectural design and secondly the lack of amentities and social provisions. This lack is seen particularly in the sphere of provisions for leisure activities. This absence of social facilities has, according to these critics, resulted in the lack of development of community life. The absence of a separate 'community life' for these areas has been seen as the cause of a whole range of social problems which have been found within *les grandes ensembles*, from dissatisfaction among the residents at the lack of unplanned open space and poor shopping and commercial facilities to juvenile delinquency. This reaction against lack of provisions has led to the formation of residents' associations who are seeking a share in the running of the neighbourhood. This type of 'community' emergence is similar to that found in British estate studies and formulated as the 'phase hypothesis' of community growth.

Les grandes ensembles of France have not provided new 'communities' in the sense of areas with an independent social life due to their limited conception of their purpose, to provide accommodation for people rather than a new social environment. Nor is there likely to be much of a 'community' in terms of shared expectations and meanings built up through interaction within the locality, due to the commuting nature of the work and the familial structure. *Les grandes ensembles* in many ways illustrate one of the constant themes of urban development, the conflict between the individual's aspirations, the shortage of accommodation and architectural and planning styles; the housing shortage and demand for single-family accommodation being one part of the question, the other being the modes of meeting this shortage currently in vogue. The influence of the architect/planner Le Corbusier is here of importance as his conception of building multi-storey residences of modern materials as an answer to the problem of housing people in the present age can be seen in the development of *les grandes ensembles*. Although Le Corbusier, himself, envisaged the creation of total new environments through the use of modern technology in the building of multi-storey dwellings, it has in practice been his architectural style rather than his social philosophy which has become an integral part of the mid-twentieth-century housing and urban scene.[33] It would appear that these new developments of France have created a new social environment with a new set of social problems which will have to be ameliorated over time.

IV   SUBURBAN

The United States has in many ways been the home of suburban literature and studies and has provided most of the data to stoke the fires of the suburban mythology.[34] However, behind the myths there does lie substantive research which allows a picture to be developed of the characteristics of these 'new American communities'.

They are privately developed, often at the scale of new towns in the United Kingdom (e.g. the Levittowns of Long Island and Pennsylvania)[35] and are the homes of middle-class white Americans. They have been developed at fairly generous densities with the average plot being between one-quarter and one-half acre of land. The individual has a degree of choice of site and house, the main constraint being that of income which is fairly powerful and means that suburbia is only possible for middle and upper income groups. The typical suburban family is seen as a nuclear family unit with young children and this characteristic is seen to give them their cohesion and visible homogeneity. The recruits to the suburbs are mostly from city areas where the families were living in privately rented property which was large enough for their needs but was probably in an area which was declining in its social status and so in its acceptability to families with rising incomes experiencing upward social mobility. One important feature has been the high social and geographic mobility among the sections of the population who live in the suburbs with an annual turnover suggested as high as 25 per cent of residents per annum. This turnover has consequences for both the stability of the suburb and the structure of its social relations.[36]

The suburbanite is seen to place great stress upon home ownership, upon his children and upon his occupational success.

Gans,[37] one student of suburbia, considers that there are differences between the United States suburbs, depending upon their class composition, with the home centredness being much more common in lower middle-class suburbs, where it is an essential part of the particular class culture. This leads to some of the areas of controversy regarding the structure of relationships and activities in the suburb. Some writers have stressed the high level of satisfaction with the suburb by the residents, have found high levels of social participation of both a formal (in clubs and societies) and an informal type (in *kaffee-klatsch*, lawn and barbecue parties). They have described a 'trusting and open' attitude towards neighbours as the dominant note and high levels of 'communal activities'. Others, on the other hand, have found evidence of a 'domestic ethic' and limited activity outside the family. The answer here may well lie in the range of type of suburb which exists, thus the likelihood of more than *one* pattern of activities being found.

The characteristics of the suburban family which is shorn of its supportive kinship linkages are considered to be one of the causes of the 'suburban problem or neurosis'. This arises from the uniformity of design and age of the housing stock which leads to areas having a predominance of young families passing through the same child-rearing stages at the same time. This, together with the long commuting times of many fathers, leads to the mother having the major role in child rearing and spending virtually all her time in a child-centred and dominated world. This is so within the home and also often when she goes out it is to play centres or *kaffee-klatsch* where the discussion is of the children and child-rearing theories. This limited world and captivity within the suburbs can lead to feelings of boredom, frustration and loneliness.[38]

The attention of many of the studies has been focused on particular areas of behaviour change which have been attributed to suburban living. These are friendship patterns, religion and political allegiances and community conflicts. The pattern of friendship has been shown to be important and is based on spatial proximity. This, it has been claimed, suggests that status distinctions within the suburb are not important. All the residents of a given area are defined as of similar status therefore status striving would not be a within-suburb activity but would if it existed, refer to the individual's relationship to reference points and groups outside the suburb. This contention is again one which is subject to divergence of views, as, for some, suburban areas are the centres of this kind of status competition.

In respect to religious behaviour there was the suggestion that suburban areas had exceptionally high rates of religious participation. This was seen in part as a function of the churches' community role in a situation where ties were weak between individuals and they needed an organisation to provide the framework within which they could find and establish personal relationships. The evidence here would suggest this is class based in that it is the middle-class suburbs with the highest rate of activity which have the highest rate of religious participation. Consequently, this change where it occurs is class, and perhaps mobility based rather than suburban.

The evidence regarding political party affiliations is not entirely convincing and here the argument was that suburban residence was associated with Republican voting. This was again due to upward mobility leading to adoption of new reference groups and also to the acquisition of property which was considered to induce greater conservatism.

Lastly, the question of sources of tension within the suburban community has been examined. The most common source has been regarding the content of and the financing of education. The new suburban dwellers moving into an existing township with its school provisions, because of their family structures, soon create pressure upon the existing school system which has to be expanded or new schools built. This requires finance and the levying of increasingly high local taxes as the suburban developments continue. This creates tension and conflict between the original inhabitants of the township and the suburban dwellers as the former's tax levels have been forced up and they may well be receiving no benefit as their children may have been through the school or they may not have children at all. The second source of conflict has been regarding the content of the education and here the role of the parent–teachers' association has been of considerable importance. The new suburban middle class have often more progressive ideas and are willing to push them strongly via the PTA. This often brings them into conflict with the existing school authorities and original inhabitants. The new methods and educational programmes often demanded by the middle class are also often more expensive, so this latter also places pressure upon the local tax rates.[39]

V   COMMUTER VILLAGES

Commuter villages are part of the urban decentralisation process as are suburbs. In fact they have tended to be called 'reluctant suburbs'[40] in America rather than commuter villages. They are the villages on the peripheries of the city which have, over time, been changed by new development, principally for daily commuters to the near-by city. The commuter village, unlike the suburb, still retains a considerable village population. As methods of transport have improved, the distance of these commuters from the urban centre has steadily increased. For example, in America an area developed in the 1950s was 36 miles from the city centre,[41] whereas current American examples are up to 100 miles from the centre.[42] The growth of the commuter village has been particularly marked in the post-1950 period. Between 1921 and 1966 cities in Britain grew by 10·7 per cent, urban districts by 72·8 per cent and rural districts by 123·1 per cent.[43] Most of this rise was the result of the growth of commuter villages. To take two urban areas as examples, Moindrot shows that for Birmingham, between 1951 and 1961 80,000 people left the city for peripheral towns and for the rural district of Warwick 33 per cent growth, Meridon 51 per cent and Seisdon 70 per cent.[44] The second relates to the growth around Nottingham. Here in the rural district to the east of the city, population grew between 1951 and 1966 by 94 per cent and in the villages nearest to the city by as much as 240 per cent.[45]

The reasons for the move to these villages related to housing and employment. For many these were the areas where new housing was available at the price they could afford. This is shown particularly by studies of developments in Kent.[46] There were also those who moved into them as they were seen as 'nice places', but this was mainly into the more exclusive upper middle-class commuter villages. For most the move was for a house rather than the area and they were drawn from the urban area, and the majority were middle and lower middle-class people. They were also, like suburban populations, nuclear families, usually with small children; one study found 93 per cent of the families of this type. The role of the wider kinship system was seen as supportive in an economic way, in loans for housing, assistance in careers, children's education, etc., rather than through visiting.

The predominant finding of studies of these communities has been the way they have developed as two separate communities of newcomers and established residents.[47] The development of the new areas within the existing village creates a new physical component distinct in materials and design from the village. In many cases there have been two types of development, one through the modernisation of the older houses and the other by the building of new houses. The former type have been small in number and have often attempted to become involved in the local village life through activity in the parish council, local fêtes and church activities. Their acceptance has depended very largely upon the particular village and the attitudes of the newcomer, predominantly upper middle class, to the local customs. Where they have been accepted, it is into vacant positions within the established social structure vacated by the tradition leaders of the 'squire, parson and teacher'.[48] The latter group of newcomers are a larger and more distinct group from the existing village population, both physically and socially, with their work and interests found outside the village in the urban centres. This tendency was most marked among London commuters in Pahl's Hertfordshire study. This group of newcomers, therefore, see the village only as a dormitory fulfilling limited functions, whereas the established village population have a much longer commitment in the village and their pattern of social relationships is more likely to be centred within it and the neighbouring villages.

The pattern of segregation which emerges is one based upon social class, length of residence and commuting characteristics of the population. The separation into such communities creates ones with considerable apparent homogeneity. Studies of development of relationships within commuter villages show that neighbour relations do develop on the basis of proximity and demographic similarity, i.e. amongst young families, older couples, etc.[49] However, proximity does not emerge as the main basis of friendships. This was found to be work followed by voluntary associations and physical proximity. It has also been shown that the visiting of friends and their role *vis-à-vis* the family is more important than kinship in the higher socio-economic groups. The involvement of the commuter section in local activities does not appear extensive, rather they emerge as home-centred, preferring informal social contacts. This could be partly a reflection of their relative newness to the locality and the fact that they are mostly in the 'child rearing' stage of their family with its attendant difficulties of involvement in outside activities.

The new communities which have formed on the fringes of urban areas do appear to have a number of features which suggest a particular pattern is emerging which marks them off from developments considered in earlier sections. They are, of course, much smaller in scale and have often a more varied history of development and the residents exercised some degree of choice in their area of residence. The way of life of the inhabitants suggests one in which a separation occurs between the new and the old creating two often spatial as well as socially distinct residential areas. This arises from the differences in the occupations, place of work and involvements with organisations and individuals external to the residential area. The residents are not a cohesive social group; they place emphasis upon individual family activities and see the residential area at best as only a 'partial community'. Consequently, leisure activities are private rather than public and 'community centred' activities usually fail through lack of support. These areas have characteristics which could lead to various types of inter-group conflict. This will arise from the lack of interaction between the various constituent groups and lack of similarity in their interests and backgrounds. Conflict would be expected in such spheres as education, where it may well be found that newcomers and the local population have different values and standards regarding the local village school, although the small degree of independence of the local school in the United Kingdom lessens the likelihood of tensions on the scale of that previously mentioned in the United States where education, both its cost and provisions, has been one of the most contentious issues in the suburbs. The separation of the village into these kinds of divisions also explains why the increase in population does not necessarily lead to a revitalisation of community life through the entry of newcomers into the structure of the existing village activities.

VI CONCLUSIONS

In the countries examined and in the various types of new urban development and redevelopment there are a number of common features which are of importance. The first is the way in which the movement of individuals and families into the various types of new residential areas discussed have led to the imposition of strains and in many cases to the breakdown of one system of social relationships. The system of social relationships was usually based upon a form of extended family structure associated with residential propinquity. This breakdown was found to be associated with the failure of the residents to fully replace this former system of social relationships by an alternative one based upon either residential propinquity or other criteria.[50] This was found, however, to be to some extent class conditioned with the higher socio-economic groups like the American middle- to upper-middle-class suburbanite appearing to have established a new form of communal solidarity. The second is that in all but the Czechoslovakian case, the residents of these new developments were predominantly young married couples with children living in single-family housing. This factor in many ways is one that contributes to the problem of establishing 'communal' social relationships, due to the restrictions placed upon activity by the structure of the families. The third feature is that all the types of development considered produce partial communities in the sense that they serve only a limited number of the needs of the individual or the family, being dependent upon the near-by city centres for work, shopping and entertainment and leisure provisions. This aspect was found to be more evident in some of the developments examined, for example *les grandes ensembles* of France were designed and built to meet only one need of the family, that of housing, whereas other developments have tried to provide for wider needs of the residents through the provision of shopping areas and community centres. Lastly, the developments considered in this chapter have been for the most part what can be termed 'non-ideological' in the sense that they have not been striving to create a new social environment. Some of the developments have had a greater degree of total 'community' planning aiming to create positively, whereas other, particularly the American suburb, have been built by speculative builders who have seen their prime function as the construction of houses, not a total environment. For example, the original Levittown in Long Island began as a small development and expanded to the proportions of a new town without ever having a 'master plan', which meant that amenities like schools and so forth were not planned at the outset but added in an *ad hoc* kind of way as the development grew in size. Similarly, American urban renewal programmes originally were housing-oriented but as noted earlier have now come to embrace a more comprehensive view of development as 'community renewal'.

The residential areas examined so far have shown a trend, therefore, to social isolation and increased residential mobility and a lessening of attachment to a particular residential locale as a centre of social relationships. The planning philosophy, out of which many of these have emerged, had alternative aims in terms of the re-creation of the small-scale meaningful residential area. The reason for the apparent failure of the planners here to reproduce this conception of the 'new community' is due to a number of factors. The first is that much of the planning and design was lacking in social content in terms of construction of facilities other than housing which might provide a forum for the generation of wider social interactions. The second lies in their misconception regarding the nature of solidarity within older areas and rural communities. Much of this was due to the strength of tradition and kinship interconnections as the work of studies like Gans,[51] Lewis[52] and Young and Willmott[53] have shown. The development of residential areas of rather a restricted range of house types has effectively broken up these older patterns of mutual support and stratified the population by, among other things, age and stage in the family cycle. The third has been the tendency to underestimate the extent to which individuals seek and demand privacy, separateness and individual activity. From some of the early studies of housing estates like that of Kuper's[54] study of Coventry to the most recent, one dominant theme has been the demand for privacy. This, together with residential mobility often linked with occupational career mobility,[55] have for large sections of the population meant an elaboration of the domestic ethic at the expense of 'communal sociability'. Finally, they have placed too much faith in social engineering via improvements in the physical environment.

Chapter 4

New Towns

The development of total new communities rather than partial communities has been the driving force for the growth of new towns in Britain and in many other parts of the world in which new towns of a similar type have been created. An analysis of new towns must begin by taking into consideration their origins as they grew out of a complex process of individual and group pressures and were a reflection of particular kinds of social values. Also, because of the clearer aims which they had, they provide an opportunity for examining the way in which the actual structure of the communities has differed from that aspired to in the original plans.

I ORIGINS OF THE NEW TOWNS

There are four factors which have to be considered when examining the question of why there are new towns. First, there is the nineteenth-century legacy and disenchantment with the industrial city; secondly, the role of certain influential individuals beginning with Ebenezer Howard;[1] thirdly, the role of pressure group activity; and finally, the role of political action and the attitude of the various political parties.

The earliest hint of the idea of a garden city, which was to mark the beginning of the new town movement, appeared in a lecture, delivered by the Christian Socialist, Charles Kingsley, in 1857 entitled 'Great Cities: Their Influence for Good and Evil'.[2] This theme, then, of anti-urbanism, of rejection of the city and the impossibility of solving its problems within its own framework has found its outlet in the proposals of contemporary planning for the planned dispersion of population and control of further urban growth in London and the other conurbations. These current planning policies can, therefore, be seen to be linked to particular social values generated during the eighteenth and nineteenth centuries[3] which were to have a marked influence upon the course of urban development in the twentieth century.

The second major element in the development of the new towns which this leads us to is the role of key individuals. The first of these is Ebenezer Howard, who in his famous book, *Tomorrow: A Peaceful Path to Real Reform*, published in 1899, advocated the idea of entirely new towns which would combine the benefits of urban and rural living. Howard, himself, was not aiming in his garden cities to create rural utopias but a new kind of still essentially urban community. These communities would be ones with a balanced development not solely residential but also with a viable industrial and commercial base. This self-containment which was to be the ideal would have the advantage of reducing the long journeying to work which was held to be undesirable by Howard and would also assist in relieving industrial and population pressure upon the large and growing urban centres. This growth would also be checked by adopting policies aimed at limiting the size of the city. This aim could best be achieved according to Howard by surrounding the city with a belt of agricultural land which was then kept free of any urban or industrial development. Howard's two proposals then of the garden city and control of city size through the use of green belts were intended to prevent the aimless sprawl and ribbon development of housing in favour of planned use and urban development. Howard succeeded quite quickly in persuading enough people to support his ideas so that he was able to buy land at Letchworth and begin the first garden city there in 1902. This living experiment was very important as it provided for the supporters of Howard's ideas a living example of what could be achieved. Letchworth,[4] however, in its early days was not a particularly outstanding success. For example, the cottages constructed for the lower-paid workers to provide them with better housing than in the industrial cities, one of the objectives of the garden city, were let at a rent which effectively excluded the lowest paid manual workers. The company founded to develop the town also ran into financial difficulties owing to the too optimistic views about the period needed to recover their original investment and turn it into a profitable venture. Nevertheless, Letchworth and later Welwyn Garden City begun in 1910, played an important role in the campaign to persuade the government and others that this was indeed the solution to the urban problems of the country. After his death, Howard was succeeded, as the leading exponent of the new town philosophy, by Sir Frederic Osborn who played a key role in the growth of the acceptability of the idea of the new towns within Britain.[5] Osborn worked for this end through individual and small group contacts and as one who gave evidence to the two key commissions, the Barlow Commission and later the New Town Commission under Lord Reith which reported in 1946. Another writer who has played a very influential role in providing the intellectual rationale for the new town movement and its emphasis upon social community planning has been the American Lewis Mumford, who, although he wrote in America, has been influential in Britain and elsewhere.[6] Not only were there these individuals in Britain who were influenced by Howard's work and were either developing or pressing for new town development but there were also influential individuals in America who added to the conception of how a new town should be planned. Particularly important here is Clarence Stein,[7] a planner and architect who was responsible for an early new town in America. These, however, were not quite the independent communities that were envisaged by Howard or advocated in Britain but in fact became planned suburban communities inhabited by, for the most part, commuters. Nevertheless, Radburn, New Jersey, designed and built by Stein in 1929, has had a profound effect upon the design of subsequent new towns. Stein's intellectual foundations lay in the work of Howard and the planner Patrick Geddes together with the economic writing of Thorsten Veblen[8] and the sociological analysis of Charles Cooley.[9] Stein believed that a city should be built to give its inhabitants security and happiness and it was in an attempt to realise these ideals that he constructed his designs for Radburn. This design had a number of basic elements. First, there should be the use of both superblocks and houses; secondly, specialised roads should be planned and built instead of one road for all users; thirdly, there should be a complete separation of pedestrians and cars; fourthly, the houses should be turned around so that the living-rooms faced the garden, and finally, the town should be built with a park as its spine. This design had a number of elements which were new and genuinely innovative at this particular time but are now incorporated into many new town designs. These were the integrating of superblocks with other housing types, specialised and separate means of circulation, and the park backbone. Stein was also influenced in his work by another American who has also been important in the sphere of new town designs, Clarence Perry.[10] Perry developed his idea of the neighbourhood unit as the basic planning unit of urban design in the same period that Stein was designing and developing his plans for Radburn. Both these men have had a considerable influence, not so much upon the decision to create new towns, but upon the shape that the new towns actually took once the decision to build had been taken in the post-1945 period. In the period up to the 1940s there were, therefore, a number of influential individuals who were involved in developing the structure of the new towns or garden cities. In Britain, prominent was Raymond

Unwin,[11] one of the designers of Letchworth and Welwyn, and in America, Stein and Perry. Also there were individuals who were constantly and persuasively advocating the adoption of a new town policy as a means of solving current social problems.

The third element to be examined is that of organisations or pressure groups. Here the concept of the garden city was advocated by a group founded for this purpose by Howard in 1889, called the Garden Cities Association. This it remained until 1909 when it became the Garden Cities and Town Planning Association,[12] indicating a broadening of its concern to the control of the urban environment through planning, which it remained until 1941 when it became the Town and Country Planning Association. Garden city associations were also established in France, Germany, the Netherlands, Italy and the United States between 1903 and 1906, indicating the way in which Howard's ideas spread and found support in other industrialised countries. In 1913 the British Garden Cities Association was instrumental in founding an International Garden City Federation which later became the International Federation for Housing and Planning. The idea, therefore, of the garden city new town was from the beginning advocated not just by one individual but by a growing and informed body which by the 1940s had become quite influential and was well prepared to give well-documented submissions to the government commissions of Barlow and Reith, advocating new town and urban control policies. The main leaders of the Association were its founder, Howard, and then Osborn who filled key positions within the association until 1961 when he retired to positions of less responsibility within the Association. The Association's strategy was not that of a populist movement attempting to enlist mass public support but rather that of enlisting support of members of Parliament, business and commercial executives interested and involved in urban planning, and leading town planners. The most important professional planner, as far as the objectives of the Association were concerned, was Patrick Abercrombie who, in his plan for the post-war development of London, reflected the philosophy of the Association of control of urban growth and planned dispersion through new town development. This philosophy led the Association to be amongst the first advocates of regional and national planning. The membership figures of the Association clearly show that it has been a pressure group rather than a populist movement. For example, in 1960 the membership was about 1,400 of which 750 were private individuals, 550 local authorities and 100 were firms.

The Garden Cities Association had few allies in the inter-war period. However, in the early 1940s the Fabians began to emerge as allies of the Association as they became convinced of the need to carry out comprehensive rebuilding in the post-war period, which would involve building new communities and establishing green belts. Support also came from the Labour Government after the election of 1945 for town planning and for the concept of the new town with its underlying themes of social balance and equality. Since 1945 both these aims of national town and country planning and new town construction have been integral parts of the policy adopted to deal with the urban growth of Britain.

Just as there were these pressure groups and individuals in favour of the new towns and garden city policies there were groups opposed to these ideas. There were three of these of importance. The first group came from within the architectural profession. This group argued against the low-density housing concept of the garden cities, and for a place for multi-storey buildings within the urban area as a whole. It was also suggested that it was considerably more convenient and economical for families to live closer to the centre of cities where employment and services were currently situated than to be moved out to new towns where both employment and services had to be developed afresh. Running through this opposition to the solution to the urban problems of Howard is the influence of one of the other great influences on twentieth-century urban development, Le Corbusier.[13] This French architect and planner advocated the housing of families in multi-storey dwellings at high densities, these to be offset by placing the residential clusters amidst parkland. The second set of opponents have been the rural and agricultural preservationists and protectionists groups who have opposed the idea of the new town as it consumes large quantities of agricultural land. This opposition is perhaps paradoxical in that a well-developed new town, green belt and urban control policy as advocated would in all probability be much more able to conserve land in an effective way than the alternative piecemeal suburban developments and unchecked city growth. Finally there has been opposition from those who have not accepted the view of the Association and its allies that cities must be contained and the population siphoned off into new developments. This opposition to new town developments has been considerably stronger in other countries. In the United States, for example, the opposition of city political, commercial and business interests have effectively delayed and limited federal government initiatives on new town development.

The existence of these opposed interest groups has had the effect of limiting or reducing the impact of the pressures exerted by the Garden City and Planning Association on the political decision-makers. The way in which the new town policy in Britain gained acceptability is a good example of the way in which the creation of the urban environment is in fact produced by the conflicts between groups holding different social values which are mediated through the workings of the political system. The outcome in terms of policy depends upon the strength and influence of the particular groups. In Britain in the 1940s the Town and Country Planning Association view corresponded with that of the Labour Party and other influential groups as it seemed to offer a way of avoiding the mistakes made in urban development in the inter-war period. Osborn,[14] writing on the development of new towns in Britain, considers that the acceptance of the idea was delayed until the 1940s due to the suburban boom at the turn of the century which somewhat overshadowed the garden city and the housing drive of the 1920s and 1930s which led to the housing estates which in turn stimulated interest in the garden city as a more balanced approach to meeting the housing shortage.

This brings us to our final consideration of the political development of the new towns through government legislation. The concept of the new town as a planning ideal did not materialise until after the 1930s and was the result of the successful pressures of the individuals and groups noted above, together with a dissatisfaction with inter-war housing development and the desire to create better environments in the renewal necessitated by the wartime destruction. There were, within the space of five years, two major government commissions and the influential Greater London Plan. These together demonstrated the effectiveness of the advocacy of the Garden Cities and Planning Association and their allies and laid the foundation for subsequent town and country planning. The first of these was the report of the Barlow Commission in 1941 which advocated the creation of a new Ministry of Town and Country Planning.[15] This was followed by the report of the New Towns Commission under Lord Reith which laid down the guidelines for the first set of new towns established under the New Towns Act of 1946.[16] The Commission in its report formulated a size norm of 50,000 and an overall density norm of 15 persons per town acre and recommended the creation of a separate legislative and administrative framework for new town development. Since 1946 the size limits for the new towns have been gradually increased due to two principal factors. First, the problem of urban growth in London and the conurbations which required larger new towns if they were to have any chance at all of relieving their growth pressures. Secondly, it was found by experience that the new towns needed to be larger than the 50,000 limit originally conceived in order to provide adequate amenities and employment for all their population. The size norms were consequently raised first to 70,000 and then later to 130,000 for Harlow, Stevenage and Basildon, three of the original eight new towns in the London region. In the latest set of new towns to be designated there has been some alteration in the new town concept. The original set of new towns were sited either on small villages or towns or on entirely agricultural land with in either case small initial residential populations, therefore, all the facilities and population were brought in and developed from nothing. In the latest generation of new towns, those designated in the 1960s, some have quite a different base, being centred upon existing towns which in some cases are well established and quite large, e.g. Warrington (127,000), Northampton (131,000) and Peterborough (80,500).[17]

New towns in Britain have had a separate legal and administrative framework from other urban developments, conferred upon them by the New Town Acts and by the decision that the development should be promoted through a separate body, the Development Corporation, independent of the existing local authorities. There was also a conscious decision to build relatively small communities. This pattern has not always been the one that has been adopted for new town development. In a similarly highly industrial, urbanised country to Britain, the Netherlands, the route to a new town policy has emerged out of conflicting interest and pressure groups. In the Netherlands, the creation of new communities is linked to the creation of new land through reclamation work in the Polder Project.[18] The decision to embark upon the Polder Project shows the way in which land use is ultimately dependent upon political decision-making. Therefore, we need to analyse the complex of social power and interest group behaviour.

The original idea of enclosing the Zuyder Zee and creating new land gained support in the Netherlands through the determined pressure of a small group of interested and influential people during the nineteenth century. This group submitted plans to the Dutch Government at various times during the nineteenth century and organised themselves into an association in 1886. This was called the Zuyder Zee Association and, once formed, it commissioned a study of the project and published a plan showing how it could be accomplished. The architect of the plan and Secretary of the Association, Dr Lely, became the Minister of Transport, Water Control and Public Works in the Dutch Government and was then able to submit his plan to Parliament. This he did for the first time in 1901. It was not, however, until 1918 that he was able to achieve the passage of an act providing for the closure of the Zuyder Zee and the subsequent reclamation of the land. The original plan for the Zuyder

Zee work had four aims. These were first, to provide by means of the North Sea Dam an improvement in the protection from the sea of the areas around the Zuyder Zee. Secondly, and related to the first, it would aid in the control of drainage in the area. Thirdly, it would provide in the new fresh water lake a source of water and finally, and most important, at the time, it would provide the country with an additional 10 per cent of agricultural land. The assumption in the 1920s when the Polder scheme began was that the principal land use would be agricultural and in the first of the four Isselmeer Polders all but 10 per cent of the land was used for agriculture and only 1 per cent was used for residential development, this 1 per cent being in the form of small new agricultural villages of between 800 and 1,400 people. In the second polder to be developed, the North Sea Polder, there was the introduction for the first time of social science investigation into the planning process and the new communities planned were based in part on the results. In these studies they found that distance between outlying houses and farms and the centre of a village was five kilometres, this distance representing the area around the village within which the distribution and educational systems had developed, hence the whole of the villagers' life tended to be geared to this distance norm. The planners, using the norm, planned ten villages varying in size between 1,000 and 2,000 and one town of Emmeloord. The latter, which was the first of the polder new towns, was begun in the late 1940s and was intended as a regional centre. The building was to be 80 per cent of the houses in rows, 15·6 per cent in flats and 4·4 per cent in detached and semi-detached houses with densities of 17 persons per acre. The higher proportion of both row houses and flats is an interesting contrast to the British new towns being developed at this same time.

Since their inception there have been changes in the functions of the new Polder lands. This re-thinking of their role first appeared in the 1950s in a report which examined the problem of the increasing population of the Northern Randstad, particularly Amsterdam, the most pressing need in these areas being for more land for residential and recreational development.[19] This led to new plans being developed for the two Polders of East and South Flevoland and Markewaard which defined a new purpose for the Polder lands, of aiding in the reduction of the population densities in the Western Netherlands, of enlarging the available recreational areas and of providing improved communications. The new plans for these two polders show a marked change in land use patterns with only 50 per cent of the land now to be used for agriculture. The remaining land will be used for recreation (25 per cent) in the form of woods, etc., and 18 per cent for residential purposes. The plan envisages the polder lands taking 500,000 people by the year 2000, principally in two new cities, one of 250,000.[20] The changing pattern of land use and the decision to create new cities and so radically alter the earlier plans for the environment were taken by the government in response to new pressures and demands which were generated between 1928 and 1958.[21] Just as the original scheme had not met immediate universal acceptance, neither did the changing policy towards land use. This was because there were groups who were firmly committed to the maintenance of the polders for their original explicitly agricultural purpose. This development, therefore, like that of the new towns in Britain, shows how the emergence of decisions regarding new communities comes from a process of pressures by groups and individuals, conflicts and agreements within the political system of a country, the kinds of solutions adopted being in accord with the current social values and aspirations of influential sections of the population.

II   AIMS OF THE NEW TOWN PLANNERS

The aims of the new town planners have varied over the years from the first new town at Stevenage in 1946, but some common threads have remained in all the 'master plans' which have been published by the various development corporations. In all cases the plans have aimed at creating new communities which were complete in the sense of providing housing, employment and leisure facilities. They also were mostly built upon the neighbourhood principle. These neighbourhood units have contained a variety of housing types from small one-room flatlets to five-bedroom houses, shopping and community facilities. Stevenage, for example, was built in neighbourhood units of 10,000. The neighbourhood principle went temporarily out of favour in the late 1950s as can be seen from the design of Cumbernauld which was built at a higher density, 80 to the acre, with one centre. This, it was felt, would improve social contact and generally assist in the prevention of neighbourhood isolation which had occurred in the earlier new towns. However, this design was rejected in the next group of new towns, because first it was felt it contradicted the British desire for a house and garden, and second it was only possible in planning small towns and the Mark III versions are all much bigger with population targets of around 200,000. The neighbourhood unit in a modified form has reappeared in such Mark III new towns as Milton Keynes and Irvine. The planners have also mostly worked with some concept of social balance as a desired goal although this has had a variety of meaning. Finally, all the designs have been and are based upon the principle of traffic separation, first fully exploited by Clarence Stein's design for Radburn. To see something of the planning ideologies of the new towns more clearly, the plans for three rather different new towns will be examined, Aycliffe in County Durham, one of the earliest new towns outside of the London area, Milton Keynes, one of the newest in the south which is particularly interesting as from the outset its population target is higher than many of the existing new towns, and finally Livingston, as an example of one of the second generation of new towns in Scotland designed as a centre for regional growth.

The master plan for Newton Aycliffe was originally drawn up in 1948 and the target for population growth was set at 10,000.[22] This was substantially revised upwards to 20,000 and then in 1963 to 45,000 by the year 1977. The new towns outside the London region have not been part of a coherent plan but have tended to serve overspill and regional development functions. Aycliffe was the site of employment within a declining mining area so its development together with that of Peterlee was part of the attempt to create new jobs for displaced miners, rather than meeting the overspill needs of major conurbations. The master plan for the town was based upon five principles. These were first, that the new town should be one of compact residential development to allow the maximum number of people to live at a convenient walking distance from the central area and recreational facilities. This apparent rejection of the neighbourhood, low density principle is most likely due to the small existing target populations for the town. The acceptance of this aim has obvious consequences for the structure and density of the residential areas, which were decided to range from 80 persons per acre at the centre to 35 per acre at the periphery. The second principle was that the central area should contain the main commercial, administrative and cultural development and have convenient access to the main sports and associated facilities. The third was related to the need to integrate the proposed new developments with the existing population so that they too might share in the expanded provisions and facilities for living in the town. The fourth principle was the need to plan for the increasing need for leisure facilities within the population. The final principle was that the road and pedestrian network should allow convenient movement and access to all areas with the maximum possible amount of separation of motor vehicles and pedestrians.

In contrast to the plans for Aycliffe, plans for Livingston in Scotland[23] were based upon a regional survey which covered some eighty square miles around the chosen site for the new town. The town was planned to be both a regional centre and a receiver of

Glasgow overspill population. The town, which was designated in 1962, had as its initial target a population of 70,000. The aims of the planners at Livingston show certain differences from those of Aycliffe and again were five in number. The first of these was to provide a coherent structure for the town with its own character. The second was the well-established principle of vehicle and pedestrian separation, with 'environmental areas' within the residential districts where the movement of traffic is restricted and where a separate pedestrian system will be created. Thirdly, the aim of conserving the existing good landscape was accepted and the creation of such a landscape. Fourthly, the principle of maximum diversity was accepted within the residential districts into which the new town was to be divided. There was also to be a positive effort to achieve a balanced population in relation to age groups, family structure and employment. In this respect the plan aims to produce variety through its mixture of housing types with 10–12 per cent of the dwellings being flats and maisonettes and 25 per cent for sale for owner-occupation. This compares with only 5 per cent owner-occupation in the older Scottish new towns of East Kilbride and Cumbernauld and Glenrothes, but is lower than that aimed at in the other recent Scottish new towns at Irvine.[24] The overall densities are being planned at 9–16 dwellings to the acre, or about 30–60 persons per acre. The final principle relates to the position of the new town as a regional growth point. Because of this it is being planned as a population centre for a region with an estimated population of 210,000 in the early 1980s. Again it can be seen in these principles the influence of the Radburn plan of traffic segregation, the neighbourhood unit theory and the concepts of social balance and community planning.

The final example is that of Milton Keynes[25] to be built in north Buckinghamshire. The building of a new town in this area was first considered in 1962 and after much discussion by the relevant local authorities a designation order was made in 1967 under the New Towns Act. Significantly the plan here was for the construction of a city of 250,000 by the end of the present century, with housing and jobs for 70,000 newcomers by 1981 and for 150,000 by 1990. The large size and the rapid rate of increase is to provide accommodation for some of the projected two and a half million increase during the period in the south-east region. Since 1967, however, these projections for population growth have been revised downwards as population growth in the south-east has slowed down. This changed demographic condition has taken away part of the original rationale for the development of the city and raised questions as to the rate of growth for the projected city. The

Development Corporation which was established to carry out this development published its plan in 1970. In this plan they outlined six broad goals which the plan aimed at achieving. These were, first, to provide the newcomers to the city with the greatest possible opportunities and choice in terms of education, work, housing, recreation, health care and all other activities and services. Secondly, to provide easy movement of the population within the city through good communications which they propose to do by means of an efficient and convenient system of public bus services. Thirdly, to achieve social balance and variety within the city. Here the goal is to try to ensure that the city does not have the age group, class and occupational uniformity which, the planners of Milton Keynes observe, is often associated with similar new town developments. The achievement of balance is seen to be closely related to the housing goals of the plan to the provision of housing choice. The housing goals of the plan are stated as providing houses of quality, of providing a wide variety of sizes, types and prices to allow the relatively poor as well as the wealthy to move to the new town. Further it is proposed that no large areas of the town should be developed with houses of a similar type, size or tenure and mobility should be possible between the different types of tenure as the household needs of the individuals and families and their preferences change. The proportion of houses for owner-occupation has been set at the 50:50 figure in line with governmental directives and the overall densities for the cities have been set at eight houses per acre, with variation between six and ten houses per acre. The basis for choosing these particular figures is the Corporation's belief that identifiable current patterns of behaviour and individual and family preferences suggest there will be increasing demands for lower densities which will be nearer the current private sector norm of 10–12 per acre than that currently operative in the public sector of the 14–16 per acre. These density discrepancies between public and private sectors are seen to accentuate status differences between the various groups in the population, thus to be at variance with the housing objectives and goals of social balance of the new city. Attempts to ensure balance are also being made by the location of schools of all levels in relation to the areas of housing developments. The fourth goal was of creating an attractive city. This is to be achieved in part by using a variety of architectural styles and building designs. The fifth was to promote public awareness of and participation in the planning and development process. The final goal was that of the efficient and imaginative use of resources.

The plan for Milton Keynes shows a number of interesting features which are a reflection of the changing climate of planning which is illustrated by the development of new towns since 1946. The original plans for the new towns were for low density residential neighbourhoods of a fairly dispersed type linked to a central core of facilities with local sub-centres. The second generation of new towns moved towards more compact, higher density designs of which Cumbernauld is a good example and now in the latest group, in particular in Milton Keynes, there is a move back towards the low density, largely single family housing of the earlier type. The reasons for this change are largely those of social pressure and population demand and to achieve the idea of social balance which has featured prominently in the whole new town movement. This concept of social balance is essentially an ideal one, arising out of the values held by many of those who have supported the creation of new towns. These people have looked to the new town as a source of communities built upon the value of social equality encompassing somewhat loftier ideals than the much more mundane urban developments of the past and elsewhere at the present. The new towns, have then had aims and values associated with their growth, both as a group and as individual ventures, which indicate that they were communities created with a fairly clear idea as to the final shape they should take and the kind of social life and activities by which they would be characterised. How far have these aims been achieved in the new towns? Have they become distinctive new communities? These are some questions which can be examined in the light of the data that has begun to accumulate on Britain's new towns.

III   SOCIAL STRUCTURE AND WAY OF LIFE

In looking at the accumulated data on the new towns it is useful first to consider the question of what has led people to move into the new town. In a study of four new towns, Aycliffe,[26] Crawley,[27] Stevenage[28] and East Kilbride,[29] there is some variation, according to the group of migrants examined. If the total number of movers since 1946 is considered then a move for employment either to take up a new job or because the firm the individual works for moved to the new town, accounted for the majority of movers to all the new towns except Stevenage, reaching its highest figure of 49 per cent at Crawley. At Stevenage the highest proportion of migrants gave getting a house as the reason for the move (42 per cent). This reflects the role that Stevenage has played in London's overspill housing policy. The other interesting difference is the high proportion at East Kilbride who gave as their reason for moving, a better house and to live in a better area (29 per cent), which is perhaps a reflection that many residents here were from Glasgow. Taking the latest group of migrant studies, those entering between 1961 and 1966, then movement for a job has become in all the new towns the dominant motive varying between 53 per cent at Aycliffe to 42 per cent at Stevenage and East Kilbride. Data of a similar kind is also available regarding two of the latest group of provincial new towns at Skelmersdale[30] and Runcorn.[31] Here the majority moved not because of work but because of housing, 53 per cent at Skelmersdale and 50 per cent at Runcorn compared to 11·7 and 21 per cent who gave work as the reason for the move. This pattern clearly reflects the purpose of these two new towns as part of the overspill policy of relieving population pressures on the south Lancashire and Liverpool conurbations. The twin motives, then, for movement to the new towns appear quite clearly to be work and housing.

The objective of new town planners which has been at the forefront of much of their planning has been that of social balance and self-containment, particularly in regard to work and housing. So, it is now necessary to look at the population social and employment structures which have resulted in the new towns since their inception to see the extent to which they have achieved this balance. The predominant image of the new town dweller is of the young married couple with children. This view is broadly supported from the available evidence. The age structure of the new towns of England and Wales is shown by Table I. When this is compared to that of England and Wales it can be seen that in all the new towns the age groups up to 40 are all over-represented and those over 40 are under-represented, with this being particularly noticeable in the 65+ age group where the majority of the new towns have very small percentages of their populations. On the basis of these figures the towns with most youthful age structure were Peterlee, 77 per cent below 40, Harlow and Stevenage (74 and 73 per cent) in 1966 and in 1970. The changes between 1966 and 1971 are of some interest as they show a slight lessening of the concentration of the population into the under 40s age group and an increasing proportion in the over 65s. In 1971, however, the new towns are still clearly more youthful than the population of England and Wales as a whole. Although the high proportion at Peterlee could be ascribed to the fact that this is a new town in its early stages of development, both Harlow and Stevenage, however, were part of the original batch of new towns so have been in existence approaching twenty-five years by the 1971 census. This means that after twenty-five years they still have not achieved the goal of a balanced age structure both having a very small proportion of their population over 65 (6·6 per cent at Harlow and 3·5 per cent at Stevenage). The new towns have

TABLE I   New towns in England and Wales—age structure 1966 and 1971

Age Categories	Basildon		Bracknell		Crawley		Harlow		Hatfield		Welwyn G. City	
	1966	1971	1966	1971	1966	1971	1966	1971	1966	1971	1966	1971
0–19	39.9	39.2	39.0	38.2	40.4	37.5	42.9	40.6	38.4	36.1	36.7	35.6
20–39	28.5	29.4	29.7	30.6	27.4	27.2	30.9	28.8	27.4	26.4	27.3	25.0
40–64	25.4	24.8	25.9	25.4	27.2	28.6	22.2	25.3	28.1	29.7	28.1	30.7
65+	6.2	6.6	5.4	5.8	5.0	6.6	4.0	5.3	6.1	7.8	7.9	8.7
Year of Designation	1949		1949		1947		1947		1947		1947	

Age Categories	Stevenage		Hemel Hempstead		Newton Aycliffe		Peterlee		Cwbran		Peterborough		Washington	
	1966	1971	1966	1971	1966	1971	1966	1971	1966	1971	1966	1971	1966	1971
0–19	42·1	40·7	37·3	35·2	39·9	39·8	44·1	42·6	38·8	37·3		32·7		29·9
20–39	31·2	30·0	27·3	26·2	31·7	30·0	33·6	31·6	28·4	28·0		25·7		30·0
40–64	22·9	27·8	38·2	30·5	23·5	25·0	17·8	20·3	27·3	28·0		30·0		29·6
65+	3·8	3·5	7·2	8·1	4·9	5·2	4·5	5·5	5·5	6·7		11·6		10·5
Year of Designation	1946		1948		1947		1948		1949		1967		1964	

Age Categories	Newtown		Telford		England and Wales	
	1966	1971	1966	1971	1966	1971
0–19		36·3		34·3	31·2	25·0
20–39		18·1		28·1	24·8	28·0
40–64		29·9		27·4	31·8	32·4
65+		15·7		10·1	12·2	13·7
Year of Designation	1967		1968			

Source: Census of Population 1966 and 1971, county volumes.

attracted disproportionately younger people and this has been most accentuated in their early development; currently Runcorn, one of the very latest of the English new towns, has 82 per cent of its population under 40. Turning from age to family structure, the age structure just described has a marked effect upon the family size as with a large proportion of young families there is also a larger proportion of children than in the rest of England and Wales, and fewer one- and two-person households. In the study of the four new towns of Crawley, Stevenage, Aycliffe and East Kilbride, for example, it was found that the average household size was between 3·41 at Aycliffe and 3·61 at East Kilbride. This compares with the figure of 3·0 for England and Wales. Also they found the average number of children under 16 per household was quite high varying from 1·14 to 1·47. Examining household types it was found that both small, younger (32–37 per cent of families in the new town and 21 per cent in England and Wales) and large families (18–25 per cent new towns, 12 per cent England and Wales) were over-represented and that 'smaller older households' (10–12 per cent new towns, 27 per cent England and Wales) and one person households under 60 were under-represented. An alternative way of looking at the structure of the families is by their position in the family development cycle. This was adopted for a study of new families at Runcorn. This showed that 64 per cent of the families were expanding, 29 per cent were stationary and 7 per cent were contracting. Both of these analyses of family type shows clearly that new towns do have a concentration of particular types of families, those with the head of the household under 40 with one or more children under 16. This structure creates particular kinds of pressures upon the new town both for education and for female employment which can be linked with raising a family of school-aged children. It also assists in creating the problem of the 'captive wife', limiting her mobility and helps account for the low levels of interest in and participation in formal leisure activities.

The second aspect of social balance is that of the relationship between work and housing. The ideal set, and still being set for the London region new towns by the creators of the new towns, is to have a town in which people both live and work and which is, in this sense, self-contained. This objective has been sought through two different types of policy. First, through the attempt to balance employment and housing within the town as a whole and secondly, through the allocation of houses owned by the development authority only to those who have employment within the town. The new towns have been more successful in achieving total balance of housing-employment, than the latter objective of the interrelating of work and living within the town. In a recent study Ogilvy,[32] using the 1961 census data shows that the majority of the eight London new towns have achieved a reasonable state of balance regarding employment and housing, with the exception of Hatfield and Welwyn. This he attributes to Welwyn's rather longer development and its proven attractiveness over the period to industrialists which has given it an excess of jobs over housing of 24 per cent. Hatfield on the other hand has been surrounded by employment centres which has resulted in slow internal growth in employment and a consequent excess of housing over jobs of 40 per cent. Nevertheless Ogilvy finds that the new towns of Hertfordshire (Stevenage, Welwyn, Hatfield and Hemel Hempstead), because of their conscious policy of attempting to achieve social balance, have in fact become more balanced in the ten years 1951–61 in contrast to the other towns in the county. For these older towns over the same period the imbalances present in 1951 in either housing or employment have become accentuated. The planning policies pursued have clearly had a modifying effect upon the process of urban development. However, this is only half the picture of employment balance. Do the people both live and work in the new town? In the study of the four new towns of Crawley etc., it was found that the place of work varied with the tenancy status of the household, with the highest number of workers in the town tenants of the development authority or in the case of Crawley the commission for the new towns, and the lowest number in owner-occupied houses (79–82 per cent compared to 71 per cent). There was also a difference between first and second generation new town residents. Of the second generation residents living in owner-occupied houses the number working in the town dropped to 61 per cent. From Ogilvy's study of the London new towns he found that the proportion working outside the new town and living in it varied between 23 and 40 per cent with the exception of Hatfield which with 62 per cent was by far the least self-contained of the London new towns. As well as the outward movement of new town dwellers there is also the inward movement of people living outside who work in the new town. The majority of outward movement to work found in the various studies was not to central London, but to areas within a ten to eleven mile radius of the new town.[33]

A number of points of particular importance emerge from this data. These are, first, the relationship between owner-occupancy and work outside the new town and the generation effect. In the latest new towns being developed, the proportion of owner-occupier is to be much higher, at least up to 50 per cent, than in the earlier new towns. If the trend apparent above is continued it will be even more

TABLE II *Socio-economic structure—new towns—males only*

1961–1966

Categories	Basildon 1961 %	1966 %	Bracknell 1961 %	1966 %	Crawley 1961 %	1966 %	Harlow 1961 %	1966 %
Registrar Generals								
1 and 2	5·4	6·0	8·0	9·0	8·9	10·0	8·4	10·3
3 and 4	2·5	3·3	8·6	8·7	5·8	7·7	7·9	6·8
5, 6 and 7	16·8	17·6	19·3	19·6	22·7	22·7	17·9	19·2
8	4·6	5·3	2·9	4·3	3·9	3·8	4·0	4·8
9	25·0	33·8	34·7	32·7	37·2	33·5	37·8	34·5
10	20·3	22·2	14·9	15·4	11·9	13·4	13·6	14·9
11	10·3	7·1	4·7	5·2	5·3	4·9	6·7	4·1
Year of Designation	1949		1949		1947		1947	

	Hatfield 1961 %	1966 %	Hemel Hempstead 1961 %	1966 %	Stevenage 1961 %	1966 %	Welwyn Garden City 1961 %	1966 %	Newton Aycliffe 1961 %	1966 %
1 and 2	—	7·6	7·1	10·1	9·6	8·4	14·5	11·4	11·9	5·8
3 and 4	3·2	6·7	1·0	6·7	—	7·5	—	10·9	4·2	4·2
5, 6 and 7	25·8	20·2	15·3	18·0	23·8	22·9	27·3	24·8	18·9	19·2
8	—	5·0	3·1	4·6	4·8	3·9	—	4·2	4·5	8·4
9	22·6	37·1	19·4	33·9	19·0	33·9	9·1	27·8	28·7	37·7
10	16·1	13·8	27·4	17·1	16·7	16·3	7·3	14·4	26·2	18·5
11	12·9	6·4	10·2	5·7	11·9	4·4	12·7	4·3	5·6	4·2
	1947		1947		1946		1948		1947	

	England and Wales 1961 %	1966 %		1961 %	1966 %
1 and 2	9·5	9·8	9	31·6	31·5
3 and 4	3·8	4·5	10	14·7	14·6
5, 6 and 7	17·4	18·1	11	8·3	8·3
8	3·3	3·6			

Source: Census of Population Economic Activity tables 1961 } Census
1966 }

1961–1966

Categories	Peterlee		Cwmbran		Corby		Skelmers-dale	
Registrar	*1961*	*1966*	*1961*	*1966*	*1961*	*1966*	*1961*	*1966*
Generals	%	%	%	%	%	%	%	%
1 and 2	3·7	5·5	1·5	7·2	3·6	4·4	—	4·1
3 and 4	3·4	2·8	1·5	5·1	2·4	2·6	—	3·9
5, 6 and 7	14·2	17·2	10·8	15·0	11·3	12·0	—	12·6
8	7·3	5·1	4·6	6·8	4·1	4·1	—	5·4
9	40·3	38·2	18·5	30·5	45·8	42·5	—	35·6
10	21·7	19·6	23·1	21·6	17·2	17·6	—	15·7
11	5·9	7·8	18·5	9·3	12·9	15·4	—	13·4

Year of Designation	1948		1949		1950		1961	

	Redditch		Runcorn		Washington		Dawley	
	1961	*1966*	*1961*	*1966*	*1961*	*1966*	*1961*	*1966*
	%	%	%	%	%	%	%	%
	—	10·2	—	5·6	—	4·5	—	4·5
	—	4·1	—	5·6	—	1·9	—	1·2
	—	13·8	—	14·4	—	12·4	—	7·5
	—	3·7	—	4·7	—	4·7	—	4·7
	—	36·9	—	33·4	—	37·7	—	47·7
	—	20·7	—	24·3	—	27·6	—	20·4
	—	5·7	—	8·6	—	6·8	—	12·5

	1964		1964		1964		1963	

difficult in the future to achieve balance and self-containment in the sense of people living and working in the same new town. Yet this is still the expressed policy for the development of current new towns. The generation effect noted above with respect to the smaller number of second generation owner-occupiers working in the town will also increase the difficulty of achieving balance if it is a trend that continues to develop. Further, the means used to achieve the interrelation of housing and work, the home allocation policy, only has an initial effect as it does not control the subsequent employment choices of the individual or the other members of his family.

The consideration of place of work leads to focusing attention on the socio-economic structure of the new towns. From the 1961 and 1966 censuses it is possible to compare the various socio-economic structures of the new towns (see Table II). From this it can be seen that, on the whole, new towns have at least one-third of their work force in skilled manual employment which is slightly higher than for the rest of England and Wales. When the structure is examined in manual, non-manual terms, then the eight London new towns have the highest proportion of non-manual employment with Welwyn both in 1961 and 1966 having the highest proportions of these types of work (42 and 47 per cent) followed by Crawley which also topped the 40 per cent mark in 1966. In contrast to these new towns are those of Cwmbran and Corby with much smaller proportion of their population in non-manual work (14 and 17 per cent in 1961 and 27 and 19 per cent in 1966). Comparing the new town structures to those for England and Wales (Table III), then in 1961 five of the new towns, all in the London area apart from Aycliffe, had more non-manual workers than the average for England and Wales (30·7 per cent) and seven fell below this line with Cwmbran having the smallest proportion. In 1966 the number above had increased to seven, but these were now all original London new towns, with the exception of Basildon. Other points of interest are the smaller proportions of employers and managerial occupations in the new towns than the average for England and Wales and rather more professional workers, and other grades of non-manual work. The low numbers of non-manual workers in the case of Corby and the very high number of skilled manual workers is a reflection of the dependence of this new town upon the steel industry. London new towns are also better placed than the provincial ones to attract office development displaced from central London by government and local authority policies, of decentralisation. The resulting picture of the socio-economic structure of the new towns does indicate certain imbalances. In the newest new towns and in Corby there is a low proportion of non-manual work and this may be rectified in the

TABLE III   *New towns arranged according to the proportion of non-manual workers (male) in 1961 and 1966*

1961	%	1966	%
Welwyn	41·8	Welwyn	47·1
Crawley	37·4	Crawley	40·4
Aycliffe	35·0	Stevenage	38·8
Harlow	34·2	Bracknell	37·3
Stevenage	33·4	Harlow	36·3
England and Wales	30·7	Hatfield	34·5
Hatfield	29·0	England and Wales	32·8
Bracknell	27·9	Hemel Hempstead	32·8
Hemel Hempstead	23·4	Aycliffe	29·2
Basildon	21·7	Redditch	28·1
Peterlee	21·3	Cwmbran	27·3
Corby	17·3	Runcorn	25·6
Cwmbran	13·8	Peterlee	25·5
		Skelmersdale	20·6
		Corby	19·0
		Washington	13·2

course of development but shows that at least initially employment in the provincial new towns tends to be predominantly for manual workers. The concept of social balance may mean different things in terms of socio-economic structures, it may mean that in the town there ought to be a reasonable variety of employment as between levels of skill and type or it could mean something rather more ideological. In this latter sense balance has been taken to mean representative of England and Wales, so that the new town was a microcosm of the total population. If this were the case then the figures indicate a considerable amount of variation between the actual structure of the new towns and the ideal as dictated by this notion of social balance. Social balance in this latter sense is presumably extremely difficult to achieve except through housing policy, which has been unable to achieve a much more simple kind of balance, that between living and working in the new town. It would consequently be unlikely to be effective in bringing about this second and more complex type of balance.

The concept of social balance has also had an influence upon neighbourhood planning. The neighbourhood unit of the early new towns was conceived of as a balanced unit in respect to population and socio-economic type and amenities and it was anticipated that these units would become significant for social relationships. However, evidence from neighbourhood studies conducted during the 1950s showed that areas of 5,000–10,000 used in the new towns were not meaningful ones for the development of social relationships.[34] They were consequently discarded in plans for later new towns which tended to be built to higher densities to enable residents to be within walking distance of the new town centres with their wide range of services and amenities. The planning concept which at this time appeared to replace that of neighbourhood being that of 'amenity' and convenience planning. It was also believed that higher densities would aid in fostering social relationships as it increased the likelihood of social contacts. However, there has been a shift back to the residential/neighbourhood unit planning in the design of the most recent new towns and with this return once again there is an emphasis on the concept of social balance as a planning objective. The residential units have been reduced in size to around the 4,000–5,000 mark and are now related to the catchment area of the primary school. These residential units are then to be further divided into sub-units of some 300–600 houses, however, this size being the one which it is considered is large enough to 'provide choice of contacts, friends, neighbours, but is not too large to be a separate social entity and foster class distinctions'.[35] It is not always clear in such planning decisions how much consideration has been given to the attitudes and values of the likely residents of the new towns. It appears the planners have been strongly committed to certain views as regards the nature of the urban society that should be produced. Clearly they place a high value on social equality, balance and sense of 'community', which is represented by social intercourse at a local level. However, the unit sizes that are being produced and these ideas may be at variance with those of the prospective residents. It is difficult because of the lack of adequate data to be able to examine fully the relationship between planners and planned in the new town context. Two pieces of research evidence do, however, throw light upon the question. Lee,[36] in a study of people's conceptions of the idea of neighbourhood found that the majority could delineate such an area and that these seem to fall into a number of different types. These were the 'social acquaintance neighbourhood' where the boundaries were set by social interaction between individuals. The homogeneous neighbourhood, which appeared to be the most common in areas of lower middle-class and upper working-class families. The definition of the neighbourhood was given here in terms of 'people who live in houses like ours'. The last type was the unit neighbourhood and this presented one of a much more heterogeneous nature. The effects of these applied to new town planning ideas of mixture and balance would be that even with house and population mix there would still tend to be a distillation of the groups along the lines of social acquaintance (i.e. people like us) and housing types which usually means socio-economic status, unless there are no differential rents or prices. Both these factors would tend to work against the attainment of the ideal equalitarian aspects of the notion of social balance. The second piece of research is that of Heraud[37] who has demonstrated this kind of process at work in the new town of Crawley with the progressive development of greater homogeneity within the different areas of the town along the lines of socio-economic class groups.

The final aspect of the new town is that of the structure of social relationships at both the neighbourhood and town level and the leisure activities of the residents. This particular aspect lacks the comprehensive data that it is possible to examine in respect to age, socio-economic status, etc.; much that has been written and commented upon has not been adequately based upon substantive research. Typical kinds of comments have been the lack of provisions for teenagers and the so-called 'new town blues' because of the time lag between the development of housing and the provision of a varied set of amenities. Some aspects are, however, worth examining in more detail. These are those of informal activities, i.e. friends, neighbours, relations, and formal activities, i.e. participation in organised leisure activities. In the new towns there has been rather low proportions of families with relatives also living in the new town. This particular feature has been most pronounced in the early stages of their development. In a study of Skelmersdale, it was found that only 4·3 per cent of the surveyed population had parents living in the town, 4·9 per cent aunts or uncles, 18·5 per cent sisters or brothers and 7 per cent children living in separate households.[38] The same study also looked at the question of friends made in the town since arrival apart from street neighbours. Here it was found that 25 per cent had many friends, 35 per cent few and 37 per cent no friends. Further they found that 18 per cent appeared to have neither a friend nor relative in the town. This pattern of relatives and friends is a reflection in part on the family and age structure of the population and in part of the new town policy of jobs leading to housing which discriminates in favour of the younger age groups. This had been the case except in cases where whole firms have moved to the new towns bringing with them a substantial number of their former employees. The Development Corporation at Runcorn has in fact attempted to ameliorate these influences by its policy of offering houses to over 40s from north Merseyside even if no member of the family worked in Runcorn.[39] The family and age structure also has consequences for the promotion of formal leisure activities in the form of clubs and associations. For example, in the Skelmersdale study they found 70 per cent of families were not members of any club or society and in a study of families in Runcorn 83 per cent were not members of any leisure activity. This pattern of non-involvement was also found in the Skelmersdale study in clubs for children, although here there was higher involvement than amongst parents, with 68 per cent of children under 12 not in any club and 55 per cent of teenagers. In the Runcorn study they also examined the leisure activity of the families during one particular week (Easter week, 1969). From this they found that the most popular activity within Runcorn had been visiting friends (38 per cent), this was followed by church attendance (23 per cent), pubs and clubs (17·8 per cent) and the cinema (10 per cent). Outside of Runcorn they found again that visiting friends and relatives seemed to be most popular (16 per cent) followed by driving for pleasure (12 per cent) and pubs and clubs (4 per cent). These various figures, admittedly from only two new towns, do suggest very strongly that the residents are primarily family centred and 'domestic' in terms of their social activities so it is not necessarily poor amenities, as has been suggested by some, that leads to low levels of 'communal' activity. These low levels are a function of family size and age characteristics of the population, and also possibly the more conducive house and environment in which to spend their leisure without the need for external provisions and activities.

The other influence upon the shape of the community is the generation of groups within the community which have an influence upon the development of the town such as neighbourhood and residents' associations and other similar pressure groups. These groups may well emerge out of conflict with the current 'authority structure' whether this be that of the development authority or the local government authority. An example of the way in which this kind of process can modify the development of a new town is provided by the development of Stevenage,[40] particularly in its early stages. The site chosen for this new town was a small town made up of London commuters and traditional agriculturalists. At first there were quite good relations between the various groups involved in the new town development, the Development Corporation, the Local Council and the Ministry of Town and Country Planning. However, over time there developed rifts and conflicts between local residents who formed themselves into a protection association and the Development Corporation and Ministry, this led to the slowing up of the development plan for a period of time. The conflict can here perhaps best be seen as one between the rural conservativism of the original Stevenage residents and the new town concept of the Development Corporation with its features of neighbourhood planning and social balance. This same kind of problem is arising with the development of the new wave of towns being developed under new town orders but which are already large urban communities. In Warrington, for example, an existing town of 130,000, the reaction to the development plan published by the new town Development Corporation in 1972 has provoked the formation of residents' associations within the existing town to fight features of the plan which will directly affect them, e.g. residents threatened with compulsory purchase orders to make way for the new improved city centre. In this kind of situation, the development plans will be much more affected by the participation and involvement of the population than earlier new town planning sites with relatively small numbers of original inhabitants. Thus the operation of pressure groups and their resolution is likely to be more important in determining the shape of the new towns that are created.

IV   NEW TOWNS OF BRITAIN—CONCLUSIONS

The new towns of Britain originated in a particular social philosophy and a particular set of circumstances which provided ideal conditions for this philosophy to gain acceptance. Their success has been the subject of wide disagreement depending upon the hopes or ideals that the particular groups have held. One critic of the new towns has suggested that in them 'we are trading the humanity and richness of a living city for a conceptual simplicity which benefits only the designers, planners, administrators and developers'.[41] This is in part attacking the implicit anti-urbanism in much of the new town movement which has its origins in Howard and the early garden city enthusiasts and still finds its echoes in much contemporary thinking. The new towns have only had limited success in achieving their express purpose of contributing to the control and relief of the population concentration in London and the other conurbations, the London new towns taking only about 18 per cent of the growth in population in the south-east, and after twenty years or so only contain 1 per cent of the population. They have succeeded in the limited objective of balancing total employment with total housing and this has been in marked contrast to the other towns in their regions. However, they have been less successful in creating particular kinds of new communities, ones which were to represent certain ideals of social balance, equality and self-containment.[42] On most of these the planners have not succeeded in fulfilling their declared objectives principally because the individuals who migrated to the new towns have not shared their conception of what the new community should look like and be. They have brought in their own varied ideas and this has provided a much more diversified pattern not necessarily in accord with the original planning conceptions. In particular because of the population characteristics there has been a predominance of young families in the child-rearing part of their cycle which has given rise to an emphasis upon domestic ethics and styles which are also characteristic of suburban areas. Also the fact that the newcomers did not share the ideal of social balance and intermixture has meant the tendency for the new towns to become stratified in terms of residence and social groupings in a similar way to other urban areas. Without the underlying unity of purpose which stems from shared values characteristic of an ideological community the new town is essentially a collection of individuals, more carefully planned for than in many other new development, with separate and often conflicting ideas about the nature of the ideal community, which leads to many different patterns of activity within any one residential area. As an example of physical planning they have been far more successful than as an example of social planning, perhaps because this latter dimension has been inadequately developed within the process of creating a new town.

V   NEW TOWN DEVELOPMENT OUTSIDE BRITAIN

There are three different patterns of new town policy which can be identified. There are first, those countries which have adopted an almost identical approach to Britain; secondly, those which have developed new towns within the framework of explicit regional growth policies, and thirdly, where new town development has been predominantly outside the public sphere and not part of urban or regional growth policy.

The first case can be illustrated by new town development in Poland, Japan and Australia.[43] In Poland the Upper Silesia plan of 1953 proposed a network of new towns which would be places for the establishment of new industries and a means of controlling urban growth and therefore aiding in the decongestion of the urban centre. The policy led to a wave of new towns, similar to those of the London region in the 1950s. Since, however, attention has moved to developing existing towns. In Japan there was also the adoption of an 'Abercrombie-type plan' to deal with the growth of Tokyo, with the Capital Region Development Law of 1956 which initiated a regional planning approach to the problems of Tokyo. The plan devised created three rings in the Capital Region (up to 63 miles from Tokyo Central Station) consisting of an inner urban area, a green belt to prevent further sprawl of inner built-up areas and a peripheral area in which it was proposed to build new satellite towns to absorb industry and population and become a counter-attraction to central location. This policy was implemented via controls over industrial, commercial and residential development within the inner area.

The second policy of regional development has not had as one of its key elements the limitation of city size and the decentralisation of employment into self-sufficient sub-centres as has British policies. In France, Germany, Scandinavia[44] and latterly Japan, new towns have been developed more as satellites not necessarily balanced in employment and working population.[45] They have been built to produce a more orderly development of the metropolis around transport systems to provide good and rapid access for the commuters to the central business district which is still seen as the centre of employment. These satellites have varied in their degree of public sponsorship. For example in Scandinavia they have been private ventures financed commercially and so have been fairly high in price and rent areas. This private sponsorship has led in Tapiola, in Finland[46] to 90 per cent of its houses being sold for private ownership. The size of many of these satellite developments has also been quite small, those around Stockholm 15,000; Tapiola is 16,000. In France there has been more public involvement in the financing and new towns as part of public policy appeared with the master plan for the Paris region in 1965.[47] The new towns envisaged are again linked into the Paris metropolis but much more attention is given to the construction of the new town in terms of the creation of a local centre, leisure provisions, balance between employment and population, than was the case with '*les grandes ensembles*' of the pre-1965 period. One of the major elements in this concept of metropolitan development as a series of linked satellite cities is an efficient transport system to facilitate easy movement. In both Japan and America this has been taken up in new plans for major metropolitan areas. Japan in 1965 revised its original plan for Tokyo and abandoned the earlier concentric ring plan as it had been of limited effectiveness. The new plan has two areas, the inner city and newly defined 'suburban development area' with an outer boundary of 32 miles from the city centre. The purpose of the change is to induce the population to relocate at suitable points in the suburban area and to bring about a series of multi-function centres in this area, separated from each other by parks and open spaces. Beyond the 32 mile boundary the emphasis changes from small new towns to development of existing provincial towns, together with the idea of new cities at up to 44 miles from the centre at the end of new non-stop commuter railways.[48] These cities are to provide a means of solving current housing and land shortages which exist at present commuting distances to the centre where there is still and likely to be high levels of office employment. The new cities would have to be of around 300,000 to make the construction of new railway lines an economic proposition. Currently Tama new town and the new garden city near Tokyo are already planned at this new scale of new town operation. A city of 300,000, it is argued by Japanese planners, is large enough to provide some industry, cultural facilities, amusements, health services and good quality education. The North-East Illinois Planning Commission[49] have produced a similar plan for dealing with the growth of Chicago after 1975. This growth would be concentrated into four or five cities or clusters of communities of about 1 and 2 million located in the outer counties of north-east Illinois some 35–40 miles from the city centre. The new cities would have multi-purpose centres with employment but the central business district of Chicago would continue to be a major source of employment. The new centres would be linked to Chicago by efficient transport systems. A final aspect of the use of new towns in regional development is seen in their role in aiding in the development of particular regions, rather than in connection with metropolitan centres. For example their growth in Hungary and the USSR in connection with the industrialisation of previously rural region, and in Australia as an attempt to develop areas away from major coastal cities and in New Zealand as an attempt to halt the northward drift from the South Island.

The final area of new town development which is of note is that in the United States where the advocacy of new towns as part of comprehensive urban and regional planning has met with little real success and such new towns as have been built are private ventures promoted by individuals and financial institutions. As this has been the pattern the new towns like Reston and Columbia have been mainly for middle to upper middle income groups.[50] Both Reston and Columbia have been conceived as self-sufficient communities of 75,000 and 110,000 final population designed as a group of small village-like communities with separate sub-centres linked together in one main town centre. In their design they are, therefore, closer to the British model than that of the European linked satellite development. The advocacy of new towns on a wider basis as an integral part of American urban and regional planning has stressed a number of objectives amongst which are control of urban growth and its redirection into new settlements in which the virtues of the small-scale community can be rediscovered. Further a comprehensive policy would make more efficient use of land, and house building capacity. Despite this persistent advocacy, however, apart from the private initiatives and a certain amount of governmental support for the idea no real new towns policy has emerged as an integral part of policies to either control or redirect city growth or the promotion of development in relatively underdeveloped regions. One of the reasons for this could lie in the relatively large amounts of land still available together with the short urban history which makes many of American cities in European terms 'new' urban centres.

New towns outside of Britain have, therefore, been used as instruments of policy aimed at giving control and direction to urban growth with less emphasis being placed upon them as new social environments. Consequently they have not produced radically different kinds of communities to those which have emerged in suburban areas, with low internal self-sufficiency and high dependency upon the neighbouring city for employment and services.

Chapter 5

Transitional Urban Communities

I   NATURE AND GROWTH

The pace of urbanisation and the shortage of permanent housing provided by either public or private enterprise at a price that the poorer sections of the city population can afford has led to the creation of 'transitional urban settlements' or squatter housing. Squatters are those who have no legal title to the land that they occupy. These areas may or may not be 'slums'. The increase in this type of housing has been dramatic in the majority of the developing countries, where acute shortages of capital have led to a very limited amount of public housing. In 1970 the United Nations General Assembly received a report on 'Housing, Building and Planning',[1] which gives an indication of the proportions of the population in the developing cities of the world who live in 'slums and uncontrolled urban settlements'. These figures (Table IV) show that in all cases where data is available for a period there has been considerable increases in this type of urban development. For example, in Ankara the proportion of the population in such developments has risen from 47 per cent of the city population in 1965 to 60 per cent in 1970, or in Lima from 21–36 per cent, Mexico City from 14 (1952) to 46 per cent in 1966. So the trend is firmly upwards. These figures can be taken in conjunction with the figures for the growth of the urban populations in the less developed regions of the world (Asia, Africa and South America). In these regions the urban population was 43·5 per cent of their total population in 1960. This is projected to increase to 66 per cent by 1980.[2] As this figure rises then so will the proportion of squatters to city population if the present trends continue. In many of the cities in the developing countries the position will soon be reached where the squatter population is larger than the 'normal' population. This position has already been reached at Ankara (60 per cent), Izmir (65 per cent) in Turkey, and in South America, at Recife and Maracaibo they are 50 per cent and in Brasilia and Mexico City they are rapidly approaching 50 per cent.

TABLE IV   *Extent of slums and uncontrolled settlements in various cities in developing countries*

Country	City	Year	City population	Pop. in slums and uncontrolled settlements Total	as % of city pop.
Africa					
Senegal	Dakar	1969	500,000	150,000	30
Tanzania	Dar-es-Salaam	1967	272,800	93,000	34
Zambia	Lusaka	1967	194,000	53,000	27
Asia					
Afghanistan	Kabul	1968	475,000	100,000	21
Ceylon	Colombo	1953	—	1,347 (D.U.)	
		1963	69,500 (D.U.)	30,500 (D.U.)	
China (Taiwan)	Taipei	1966	1,300,000	325,000	44
India	Calcutta	1961	6,700,000	2,220,000	25
Indonesia	Djakarta	1961	2,906,000	725,000	33
Iraq	Baghdad	1965	1,745,000	500,000	25
Malaysia	Kuala Lumpur	1961	400,000	100,000	29
Pakistan	Karachi	1964	2,280,000	752,000	25
		1968	2,700,000	600,000	33
Philippines	Manila	1968	(less than) (3,000,000)	1,100,000	27
Republic of Korea	Seoul	1970	440,000 (D.U.)	136,550 (D.U.)	35
Singapore	Singapore	1966	1,870,000	280,000	30
					15

Country	City	Year	City population	Pop. in slums and uncontrolled settlements	
				Total	as % of city pop.
Europe					
Turkey	Ankara	1965	979,000	460,000	47
		1970	1,250,000	750,000	60
	Izmir	1970	640,000	416,000	65
North and South America					
Brazil	Rio de Janeiro	1947	2,050,000	400,000	20
		1957	2,940,000	650,000	22
	Belo Horizonte	1961	3,326,000	900,000	27
	Porto Alegre	1965	872,000	119,799	14
	Recife	1962	680,000	86,465	13
		1961	792,000	396,000	50
	Brasilia	1962	148,000	60,000	41
State of Guamabara		1950	2,240,000	159,000	7.1
		1960	3,300,000	337,000	10.2
Chile	Santiago	1964	2,184,000	546,000	25
Colombia	Cali	1964	812,810	243,840	30
	Buenaventura	1964	110,660	88,530	80
Ecuador	Guayaquil	1968	730,000	360,000	49
Mexico	Mexico City	1952	2,372,000	330,000	14
		1966	3,287,334	1,500,000	46
Panama	Panama City	1968	373,000	63,000	17

Country	City	Year	City population	Pop. in slums and uncontrolled settlements	
				Total	as % of city pop.
Peru	Lima	1957	1,260,729	114,000	9
		1961	1,715,971	360,000	21
		1969	2,800,000	1,000,000	36
	Arequipa	1957	117,208	10,500	9
		1961	135,358	54,143	40
	Chimbote	1957	33,000	6,600	20
Venezuela	Caracas	1961	1,330,000	280,000	21
		1964	1,590,000	556,300	35
	Maracaibo	1966	559,000	280,000	50
	Barquisimeto	1968	30,530 (D.U.)	12,518 (D.U.)	41
	Ciudad Guayana	1966	86,000	34,000	40

D.U. = Dwelling units.
Source: Taken from the Report of the Secretary-General of the United Nations: 1970 on 'Housing, Building and Planning', (Annex III, pp. 55–7, table 6).

There have been various types of squatter settlement identified. For example, Abrams[3] identified eight different types of squatter settlement, depending upon the nature of the occupancy status. These are:

1 *Owner squatters*: This is where the person owns his shack but not the land upon which it is built. This type is the most common in all developing countries.

2 *Squatter tenant*: The occupant of the shack here pays rent to a landlord who may be a 'squatter' or absentee landlord.

3 *Squatter holdover*: This is the case where a former tenant has ceased to pay rent, but the landlord is afraid to evict him.

4 *Squatter landlord*: This is the group who rent out shacks or rooms within the squatter areas, usually at inflated rents and consequently make good profits.

5 *Speculator squatter*: These are groups of individuals who practice this form of housing as a good business venture.

6 *Store squatter*: This is where an individual sets up his business on land that he illegally acquires.

7 *Semi-squatter*: This is where the individual originally acquires land illegally and builds his shack but subsequently comes to terms with the owner of the land.

8 *Floating squatter*: This is the group who live in old hulks or junks which float on rivers or within the harbour of the city.

These various categories which Abrams identifies give some idea of the variety of systems of tenure that can operate within these particular types of residential areas. They do not, however, help to identify the different types of community which are formed around the cities, which can have within them varieties of tenure. Turner,[4] from this study of South American squatter settlements has identified three broad types of squatter community. The first type is made up of people with very low incomes who are either urban born poor or migrants. They live in central areas of the city, often in tenement slums rented out at high rent levels relative to their level of income. These areas provide 'bridgeheads or urban toe-holds' enabling the poor to live close to employment and to the central food markets. The migrants are not usually direct from rural areas but have moved from smaller urban centres. The second type is populated by the families moving out of the central slum areas. The communities formed by these squatters are usually the result of an organised invasion of land either adjacent to the centre or farther out by former residents of the central city slums. They mark the beginning of social advancement for the young families with steady employment and incomes which constitute the bulk of their population. These squatter communities are termed 'low income consolidators' or 'slums of hope'. The final type is that of the 'middle-class status seekers' who are well on the way to social and geographic mobility moving on from the 'slums of hope' through progressive improvement of their housing and locality. What Turner is suggesting is a process of outward migration of the lower class from the city centre slum through acquisition of land by force and the establishment of owner occupation.

Two further studies suggest there are other patterns of development within the city which need to be considered. Oscar Lewis,[5] for example, in an examination of Mexico City, has shown how some of the migrants to the city become trapped in the inner areas by the vicious cycle of poverty and high rents. For this group there appears to be little hope of mobility socially or geographically into the wider urban society. The second by MacEwen[6] looks at a shanty town (1,168 squatters) which has developed on the edge of one of Argentine's provincial towns (25,000 population). This town was the largest within its county and was an administrative and commercial centre. Within the shanty town two groups were distinguished. The first were those who continued to work in agricultural occupations outside the town and maintain within the squatter community a traditional way of life. The second was one of families moving initially into urban occupations in the provincial centre, but still being resident in the squatter community. Then, subsequently, many taking part in movement from the area to larger urban centres and to the major cities like Buenos Aries. This emergence of two distinct patterns within the squatter settlement leads to internal differentiation in the area along the lines of mobility and involvement in urban oriented work.

The pattern of squatter settlements, therefore, has a number of elements. Prominent in this is the role of mobility both geographic and social which brings the urban oriented squatter to the large centres from the provincial shanty towns to enter the city via the 'low income bridgeheads'. Once in the city he either obtains stable work and moves out as part of the self-improvement process to the 'slums of hope' or he becomes trapped in the centre within a 'culture of poverty'.

Having identified some of the common features of the transitional urban settlements it is also important to appreciate that they also have many differences, in their physical conditions, density of settlement, community organisation and ethnic and class composition. To appreciate some of these differences it is necessary to examine a little more closely some examples of squatter communities, their formation and subsequent development. Much of the research into this type of community has been conducted in South America, consequently the first group of our examples have been drawn from work relating to Lima and Rio de Janeiro.

Squatter settlements in Lima have been studied by, among others, Turner[7] and Mangin.[8] Turner's study concerns the formation and development of a community which he calls 'Pampa de Cuevas' which was established in Lima in 1960. The population invading the area were from the city slums. They were not the lowest income group or one without experience of urban living. Many of the people had originally come from the rural areas of Peru but they had been in the city for at least ten years prior to the invasion and the creation of the new community at Cuevas. This falls, therefore, into the second category of transitional communities, that of 'slums of hope'. The creation of the community was planned and organised by a community association formed in 1959. This association planned the invasion which took place just before Christmas in 1960. The authorities at first attempted to force the people off the land, but because of the difficulties of doing this to such a large number (1,000 families), and the possibility of such a large number being homeless at this particular time of the year, they allowed the squatters to camp on part of the land as a temporary measure. This, however, became a permanent arrangement. The community association, which had organised the invasion also arranged for a survey of the area and the preparation of plans for the settlement. Once this had been completed the settlers were each allocated a plot. This method of development resulted in the squatter colony being laid out in a systematic way with roads and equal sized plots, so that the plan of the 'settlement' does not look unlike that of any new residential housing development.[9] Once the squatter families had been allocated a plot they moved their shacks and erected them on their new plot of land. Here, the aim of the squatters was to establish quickly a firm footing on the new land, as once this had been done they knew they were fairly safe because the land is rarely reclaimed by its owners at this stage. The development of these communities normally emphasises community facilities in the early phases of their development such as schools, markets, meeting-rooms, medical centres, police posts, etc., as these give to the area a stability and outward respectability which earns their acceptance by local and national governments. The means used by the squatter associations to achieve these objectives have included pressure upon politicians, the use of official services, assistance from religious bodies and the undertaking of the development themselves.[10]

Alongside the development of community facilities there is the development of the dwelling structure itself, the building of proper walls, roofs, the addition of rooms or storeys, so that over time the area develops into one of quite substantially built houses usually larger and more spacious than the government-developed new housing schemes. This process of development into permanent housing and the achievement of recognition as an established community are documented by Turner. He shows, for example, that by 1964 the government had provided a provisional water supply to the area, and that by 1965 Cuevas had become the centre of a new municipality, and in November 1966 a fully incorporated part of the city. This means that within a period of six years the community had changed from a group of homeless people in conflict with the authorities and police to a settled permanent one which had achieved formal recognition and incorporation into the city of Lima. Alongside the 'community development' there had also been an improvement in the standard of housing with permanent construction being started on 80 per cent of all the plots and by 1965 42 per cent had completed the walls of their houses to roof height. The establishment of 218 retail shops is a further indication of the stabilisation of the community. The points which emerge as important about the formation of this community are the way in which it was an organised and carefully planned community right from the preparations for the original invasion up to the present in the stress upon community development. The extent of popular participation in the development is, however, somewhat variable.

Mangin, in another study of a Lima squatter settlement, which is called 'Benavides', throws some further light upon the characteristics of members of this type of community. This community was formed through an organised invasion in 1954. Mangin found that the basic unit of social organisation was the nuclear family, with 528 out of 561 households being of this type. In 'Benavides' there existed a tenants' council which had the task of screening new arrivals and allocating plots of land to them for their occupation. This council favoured in its allocation policy, married couples rather than single women or widows with children. The tenants' association and council are the community bodies responsible for the organisation of public social life and the relations between the community and the rest of the city and city authorities. Although all the heads of the resident families belong to the association few were found to be active participants. The organisations which were found to attract most support were the regional clubs which linked together the members of the community who had originally come from the same parts of Peru. Mangin further found that the choice of neighbours as friends was not common, friends being normally found among fellow kinsmen or people from the same province of the country or were higher status acquaintances in the wider city of Lima. The community was primarily residential with the working population communting daily to the city for employment. The occupations followed within the city were found to be diverse and included both non-manual and manual employment. The characteristics that Mangin describes are very similar to ones which have been observed within suburban communities in the developed countries, with the emphasis upon home and family styles, minimal involvement in community-based activities, the segregation of residence and work and the attendant daily commuting. Finally the emergent pattern of friendships also has similarities, in that they arise out of a variety of settings only one of which is residential propinquity and this being of most importance for only a minority of the population.

Another South American country which also has large squatter development around its major cities of Brasilia, Rio de Janeiro[11] and São Paulo is Brazil. The *favelas* of Rio, for example, appear to have first developed during the 1930s due to increased migration and the high costs and limitations of the transport system in providing 'suburban' residences. The push factor was the fall in the world price of agricultural products which led to a fall in living standards in the country. This was coupled with the belief that employment and living standards were higher in the cities. The new migrants being unable either to find housing in the central rented areas or in the newer suburban areas solved the problem by developing their own housing on the steep hillsides and the vacant land which lay near to the central areas of employment. Since the 1930s the *favelas* have grown steadily in size and number as the differences between the standard of living in the rural areas and the cities continues to grow. Currently the *favelas* contain about one-third of Rio's population. This population is made up of mixed racial groups, with 38 per cent negro, 33 per cent white and 29 per cent of mixed race; also it is predominantly one of children and adolescents which indicates that the migrants were mostly younger age groups in the early stages of their family development cycle.[12] The growth of the *favelas* since the 1930s has been stimulated by further factors to that of rural–urban migration. The redevelopment of the central areas of the cities has created a surplus population to be rehoused. The public provisions were not adequate and also were at considerable distances from employment at rents which left little of the wage left after transport costs had also been deducted. Another factor has been population growth within the city through improvements in the birth rates and life expectancy. Finally the concentration of industrial and commercial development in the major cities has further accentuated the difference between the urban and rural areas and has provided further 'pulls' to the city for the rural dwellers. The *favelas*, because of their development principally by rural migrants, have been of 'rural house types', very similar to those lived in by the migrants prior to their move to the city. Within the *favela* the families are found to be largely stable units with the household heads in regular work. The key to their social organisation is in the operation of the kin groups which assists both in obtaining space or a house in the *favela* and in obtaining work. Also there exists *favela* associations which are concerned with the development of the *favela* as a whole, through such things as employment bureaux to assist in finding work, local security and policing and in some cases, levy local taxes to assist with the provision of public facilities and services.[13] However, although at one level the *favelas* of the major cities may represent a picture of adaption to urban life, community organisation and social development, there is another side to the picture. In a study of Rio *favelados* for example, it was found that the majority did not believe that life had improved for them over the previous five years and also that no one outside the *favelas* really cared or knew much about life and conditions within the area.[14] The picture of the life of the *favela* is painted much more starkly in the diary of Carolina Maria de Jesus, a woman who lived in a *favela* of São Paulo.[15] Carolina survived and fed her children through collecting scrap paper and other things from the streets of the city and selling them to scrap dealers. In her diary she describes the *favela* as the 'Garbage Dump of the City'. Her life is portrayed as one of a constant battle with hunger set against living in a community in which illiteracy, malnutrition, disease, alcoholism, violence and poverty were all around her. Also shown is the indifference of the authorities and politicians to the plight of the *favela* dweller except at election times. The *favelas* of Brazil, therefore, emerge as varied with some demonstrating progressive improvement into communities whose style of living is not unlike many other more 'conventional areas' of the city to those which are still at a level of extreme poverty with little evidence of progressive development or of a 'common will' to improvement among the dwellers themselves.

As can be seen from the United Nations Survey (Table IV), there are outside South America squatter developments in many other countries. Are these broadly the same in the range of functions they perform in respect of both the city and their inhabitants? Or are there important differences in the process of community formation and in its final composition? The table shows that squatter areas are prevalent in South-East Asian countries where the post-1945 population explosion has been the chief reason for their development.[16] One Asian country for which there is documentation on the development of squatter settlements is the Philippines, particularly the developments within metropolitan Manila. The squatter settlements here have been seen to arise out of rural migration and the effects of the Second World War upon the housing stock of the city. Also the war through bombing, etc., has provided empty sites which could be taken over and used by squatters. The growth of the squatter element in the city population has been extremely fast, trebling over the past ten years, so that Manila now has 43·8 per cent of its population in the category of squatters/slum dwellers, Quezon City 17·8 per cent and Caloocan City 13·1 per cent.[17] The first question regarding the squatter areas is what are the characteristics of the population? The home and family circumstances of the squatters are, in many respects, similar to that of the *favela* and *barriada* dwellers of Latin America. There is a clear predominance of younger age groups with 70 per cent of household members below 18 and of these 32 per cent are below school age. This reflects the fact that nuclear families with children are the basic unit within these communities. It is their need for accommodation and work to support their family which brings the families to the city and then the shortage of accommodation is a major reason for their forcible invasion of land and erection of shelters. The educational level was found to be, on the whole, low with 30 per cent having had no elementary education and only 20 per cent more than primary or elementary education. The families were also found to be living in 30 per cent of the cases in shared accommodation which usually meant sharing a single-roomed shack. Ownership of the shacks was found to be 67 per cent showing that the families had for the most part built and were living in their own shacks. The level of public utilities were found to be very limited with the majority having neither a piped water supply nor sanitation (only 25 per cent having toilets of any kind). This means that all the squatter areas were characterised by a high incidence of diseases such as cholera, pneumonia and respiratory diseases. The majority of the working population were in some kind of employment but only 50 per cent were in regular work in the docks, market or fishing industry, 25 per cent were in casual work and 5 per cent in government service, leaving 20 per cent as wholly unemployed. The greater part of the work done was, however, at very low levels of pay (less than p150 local currency) which meant that 80 per cent of the families were living at or around a bare subsistence level. The overall picture which can be derived from the data on Manila is one which suggests little variety between the squatter settlements with them all being nearer to 'slums of despair' than 'slums of hope'. There is, however, evidence of organisations within the squatters communities, with 65 per cent of the household heads being members of at least one community-based organisation. This means that they are likely to be an important political force within the city, which the politicians are unable to ignore. The existence of organisations based on the squatter communities could, therefore, provide the basis for social development in the future even if there is little current evidence of this kind of process.

Juppenlatz[18] has classified members of the country's squatter colonies into five types on the basis of his research into squatters in the Philippines. These are 'foreshore squatters' who make up about 10 per cent of the squatters in the coastal cities. Secondly, 'typhoon disaster squatters' who are those made homeless by natural disasters (30 per cent). This group very probably would have preferred to continue their previous way of life in the countryside. Thirdly, the economically depressed squatter. These are the ones who have migrated because of a lack of employment opportunities in the rural regions (30 per cent). Fourthly, there are the 'enterprising families' who are seeking improvements in their circumstances. This group have been forced into squatting by the high price of land and the limited opportunities to use their education and skills. Obviously this is the group most likely to leave the squatter communities (20 per cent). Finally, there is a group he describes as 'professional squatters' (10 per cent). These are the people who attempt to make money out of the others particularly by renting accommodation. From this analysis of types it can be seen that for 90 per cent of the squatters the move to the city and the resort to this type of community was not a choice but the result of 'push' factors and limited access to alternative types of accommodation. There was also the belief that the move would lead to an improvement in their livelihood and long-term opportunities.

The picture presented by the squatter communities of Manila does suggest some differences from the one presented on the basis of the South American data. In the Philippines the formation of the squatter colonies by planned invasion and their purposeful development as part of the social mobility and improvement of a section of the urban population is much less in evidence. This pattern may be the one associated with the 20 per cent enterprising squatters but is certainly not the norm. The growth appears less organised and the residents are overwhelmingly poor rural migrants to the city.

A variant upon the squatter colonies of South-East Asia and Latin America found in Indian cities is the 'street sleeper' who is a mobile squatter without a house who sleeps in streets, under bridges, doorways, etc.[19] It is estimated that around 600,000 such squatters are to be found in Calcutta. The existence of this type of squatter is in addition to those who illegally obtain land and erect '*bustees*' or 'tin towns'. These again are found either in the centres of the cities or on the periphery of the urban area. They are usually one-roomed shacks at very high densities without any amenities.

Another extensive study of a developing city with a long urban history which can help to display something of the development and function of the transitional urban settlements is that by Abu-Lughod of Cairo.[20] In this study Abu-Lughod divides the city into thirteen sub-cities or separate communities which have distinctive characteristics. These communities can be grouped according to the nature of their population, whether it is 'rural', traditional urban or modern industrial urban. The first two of these types represent the two original types which have a long existence in varying forms which are currently moving along different paths to a common new type of way of life termed here the 'modern or industrial-urban'. This pattern although in many aspects Western, still retains a uniqueness which differentiates Cairo from contemporary Western cities. The existence and growth of the squatter population is related to the migration into Cairo from the countryside. This movement from the country to the city began in the late 1930s and continued in subsequent decades at high rates. For example, between 1937 and 1947 the city had to absorb more than three-quarters of a million additional inhabitants. This rapid increase in the urban population led to extremely high densities in the older quarters of the city and set up pressures for expansion of the city outwards and also created pressure on vacant land within the city. Not only, however, in the post-1947 period has there been rural to urban migration to create pressure upon housing and living space but also there has been an increase in the city population through a growth in the birth rate, with three-fifths of the post-1947 growth in size being attributable to the excess of births over deaths.

In her analysis of the areas of Cairo, Abu-Lughod identifies one as having a large squatter population and possessing similarities with the *bidonvilles* of North Africa and the *favelas* and *barriada* of South America.[21] This area is the funeral quarter of the eastern fringe of the city. It is situated in the city cemetery. Here the squatter settlements have grown up with the population growing from around 40,000 in 1947 to 100,000 in 1960s. It is one which is not served by municipal services and the majority of the settlers are illegally occupying tomb houses or jerry-built shacks which they have constructed for themselves. The development of the area is becoming more formalised with the building of more substantial houses and the establishment of business and commercial activities. Over a period the area has therefore developed into a series of sub-communities, some having some connection with the area, e.g. tomb custodians, but for many it is simply a residential neighbourhood. The growth of squatting in this region has developed since the 1940s when the population of the cemetery area was around 40,000 and was mostly employed in activities within the area, either as tomb custodians or later in the lime kilns and quarries which were developed in the area. The period after 1947 saw growth in the population and the development of squatting. The reasons for this appear to be the overcrowding and housing shortages in the city produced by migration and population growth. This forced the migrants to seek cheap or free housing in the peripheral under-utilised areas of the city. This invasion then was gradual and was principally of rural migrants rather than a systematic planned invasion by residents of the slum quarters of the city, as has occurred in some Latin American cities. The migrants to the 'cemetery city' built for themselves new villages on the available open land. These new residents differed from the original residents as they were 'rural' in orientation, illiterate, poor and less well integrated into the economy of the city. Their family patterns both in terms of structure and size were closely related to rural rather than urban Egypt. The population of Cairo's cemetery city is still increasing partly due to the effects of the 1967 war with Israel and also to the continued rural to urban migration.

The data from Cairo again illustrates something of the variety in both origins, structure and style that there is amongst the squatter communities of the developing city, the Cairo communities being the first home for rural migrants to the city. This creates the 'transitional community' which enables them to change their traditional 'rural' style of living to one which is 'urban-industrial'.

One final example can be taken from Europe in which the squatters legally obtain their land but built on it without permission from the authorities.[22] This pattern of squatting has characterised the growth of Athens, particularly since 1951. During this period the rate of urban growth has been much faster than could be coped with by the authorities and each successive group of migrants has built a new belt of unauthorised housing. It has been estimated that from 1945–66, 45 per cent of the increase in Athens' total population was accommodated in these areas. The squatter settlements have a rather different development process than those already examined as the holding of legal title to the land prevents the need for organised invasions characteristic of Latin America. However, as the building is illegal it is necessary to construct the house quickly at night or on public holidays when the police and authorities are likely to be busy elsewhere. The authorities have tried to prevent these housing areas by demolition, e.g. in 1964 2,000 were demolished. The persistence of the area, however, illustrates the need for low income housing. The action of the authorities periodically to legalise whole areas, once established, also acts as an encouragement to the families to build quickly their houses. The areas have few facilities, like churches, doctors' surgeries, children's playgrounds, or amenities like sewers and refuse collection.

The areas created by the low income migrants in this case are in a state of continual development both to the houses, which are finished as money becomes available, and the areas themselves depending upon when the public authorities cease to demolish the houses and redefine them as legitimate settlements and begin to improve the public provisions. The emergence of the area is again a response by the migrants to the lack of housing. The areas, over time, will develop into conventional suburban areas with the disadvantage of a lack of overall planning in the early stages making the siting of necessary facilities for community development, like community buildings, central meeting-places in the form of shopping areas, virtually non-existent and extremely difficult to introduce.

II   THE ROLE OF THE TRANSITIONAL URBAN COMMUNITY WITHIN THE DEVELOPMENT OF CITIES

Transitional urban communities can be seen to play an important role in the development of housing, in the provision of avenues to social mobility for sections of the population, in aiding the adaptation to city life of migrants and in providing economic opportunities and employment for city residents.

The developing cities all have formidable housing problems which have arisen through the twin factors of rural to urban migration and the increased rate of population growth within the city itself. The existing housing stock within these cities has proved quite inadequate to house this increased population, in many cases it was already overcrowded before the rates of growth reached their present proportions (e.g. Cairo).[23] Also the rate and type of new housing provision has not been anywhere near sufficient to meet the increased population. The provision of housing in many developing cities has been an area of conflict between official norms and values regarding the planning and development of the city's housing and the norms and values of the population. It is possible to distinguish two distinct approaches to the housing problem.[24] The first, the traditional, sees the problem to be one of insufficient houses of a modern standard, this deficit being the result of inadequate financial and building resources. The solution is consequently the removal of the squatters and the replacement of these areas by new low income housing. One of the difficulties which arises here is the cost of providing such housing and the inability of the low income earners to be able to afford the housing when it is constructed. A recent United Nations study[25] has shown that the figure of 20–25 per cent of income usually accepted as the proportion of income available for housing by an individual family is unrealistic for low income groups, where depending upon locality, between 7 and 15 per cent is much closer to the families' available resources. The housing policies of the traditional approach further stress the importance of a modern house with proper facilities (water, electricity, sewerage, etc.) and public services as a primary goal. Once the housing has been finished, they then move to a provision of community facilities and the title to the property and the security of tenure which this brings comes at the end of the repayment period of the loan or mortgage. The low income squatters have a very different set of preferences. These are first, for a location which is close to work, schools, shops and community facilities; secondly, for security of tenure; and finally, for the quality or modernity of the house. This is the reverse of the official housing policies. The reason for this difference in preferences arises in part from the fact that the squatters are often living in central areas of rented accommodation for which they pay high rents and have no security of tenure. They also are predominantly family groups with children and, therefore, are concerned with the wider environment and provisions for their children. Their motives for squatting are also not simply shelter but are allied to a desire for social improvement.

These alternative preferences have given rise to the second approach to the housing problem, the environmental. The concern here shifts to the way the house accommodates the residents in respect to their goals and how far it provides security of tenure, and protection. The advocates of this approach believe it is only through self-help, mutual aid and co-operative schemes that large-scale housing development to meet the needs of the emerging cities can be achieved.[26] The greater involvement of the squatter in the construction and planning of his house results in squatter housing being more flexible and individually tailored than government housing programmes. Also they provide more space per family unit than do government housing norms. The standard of shelter provided in squatter areas varies enormously from some areas where steady improvement has been effected to achieve relatively good standards of accommodation to others where the standard of shelter and community facilities is very low indeed with a number of families sharing one-roomed shacks. One of the important reasons for these variations has been the role of the government, whether or not they have adopted an 'environmental' approach, as in for example, Peru, Morocco, Iraq,[27] Ghana and Tanzania. In all these cases schemes have been developed which provide some financial assistance to the family once some work has been done and a minimal foundation or 'core' of the houses completed. For example, in Ghana[28] under the 'roof loan scheme' families are able to obtain a government loan to erect a permanent roof once they have constructed the lower parts of the house.

The squatter communities, although illegal, are not necessarily sources of dissidence within the developing city and may in fact play a much more conservative role in the sense that they are firmly committed to the values of the dominant class in the wider society and have as goals, individual social improvement and educational advancement to higher status occupations in the professions and white-collar employment for their children.[29] Here, however, there is controversy between the various writers which perhaps indicates that squatter communities play a variety of roles in respect to the city in which they are located rather than just one role. The writers on squatter communities range from those who see them as constituting 'cultures of poverty' in which the residents have become trapped in a separate world and are unable to move out into the city or wider society, to those who see them as areas of transition for migrants from rural to urban society. In the view of the former writers the community rather than being a transitional one, a vehicle to mobility, becomes a permanent residential sphere of limited opportunities. This in turn brings about frustration of the residents and the development of the squatter communities as 'revolutionary cells' committed to radical programmes of reformation and change of the societies of which they are a part. For example, Franz Fanon writing in *The Wretched of the Earth* (discussing squatters in the *'bidonvilles'* of Algeria) writes 'It is within this mass of humanity, this people of the shanty towns, at the core of the Lumpenproletariat, that the rebellion will find its urban spearhead'. And, 'For the Lumpenproletariat, that horde of starving men, uprooted from their tribe, from their clan, constitute one of the most spontaneous and most radically revolutionary forces of a colonized people'.[30]

Oscar Lewis has also examined the nature of the 'culture of poverty', the encapsulated community which provides for the individual a way of life which is neither 'rural' nor 'urban', with its own system of familial relationships, characterised by consensual unions and a basic hostility to the values and institutions of the external society which they associate with the dominant class. Lewis, for example, writes of Puerto Ricans: 'Along with disengagement from the larger society, there is hostility to the basic institutions of what are regarded as the dominant class . . . hatred of the police, mistrust of Government and of those in high positions and cynicism which extends to the Church'.[31]

Lewis and Fanon, then, are arguing that such communities are distinctive and have separate systems of values and organisation to those present in the wider society. Lewis considers that the reaction is usually a negative one in the sense that people withdraw into their community and maintain their distinctiveness, whereas Fanon sees this distinctiveness as the basis of revolutionary doctrines and change.

The evidence regarding the disruptive nature of the migrants is not very strong. For example, in a voting study in Calcutta, it was found that voting in districts with heavy concentration of migrants correlated closely with Congress party voting and in a study of Chilean presidential elections a negative relationship between areas of high proportion of migrants and vote for Allende was found.[32] Other evidence suggests that urban violence stems more from middle-class sections of the population than working-class.[33] So on both conventional and more violent types of political activity there is little evidence to support Fanon's contentions regarding the revolutionary role of squatter communities.

These views are in sharp contrast to those of Mangin[34] and Turner[35] who argue on the basis of their study of Lima that squatter communities need not always be associated with 'cultures of poverty' or despair but rather can be seen as an example of self-urbanisation or improvement processes whereby families band together in a highly organised way to bring about collective upward social mobility via the creation of new communities. The pattern of life identified here within the squatter communities was one of stable family units and of associations based upon ethnic, locality and religion, for example, the caste associations of Indian cities and tribal associations of West African cities.[36] Also there were well-organised local governments with annual elections, such elections were unique to squatter communities in Peru, and a political outlook which was more conservative than revolutionary and an embracing of the value system of the city rather than rejection. Also they had achieved a modest rise in income and prospects since their arrival in the city, both in occupational terms and in having rid themselves of landlords and the inflated rents they charge for their properties.[37] Further the communities were not isolated from the city but showed evidence of a considerable volume of interaction in the form of commuting to work, attendance at schools, etc.

Linked with the involvement of the communities with the city there is the way in which they act as areas of adaptation. This again contrasts with the Fanon and Lewis view which sees them as separate and isolated. Mangin and Turner, among others, show that the population of squatter communities are not necessarily straight from the rural areas, but are ones who have had some previous experience of urban living, but nevertheless are of rural origin, the pattern being one of movement from the village to the small town to the major city. The squatter community, therefore, is part of the process of entry and assimilation to the dominant pattern of urban life. Similar evidence is found in Abu-Lughod's study of Cairo and the way in which squatter communities have arisen to provide a first home for rural migrants.[38] Also evidence comes from the way in which the *bustees* of Calcutta[39] serve a similar function by providing housing at rents the lowest income groups can afford, reception centres for migrants, employment in marginal small-scale enterprises, social and community support for the migrant as he makes the adjustment to his style of living to fit into the urban community.

Finally, the squatter communities make an economic contribution in the sense that they create work through the small businesses which grow up in the communities and in the saving to the city they provide by constructing their own housing. Further, many of the inhabitants are both workers and consumers within the city and this again has an effect upon the overall buoyancy of the city economy.

III   CONTRIBUTION TO THE UNDERSTANDING OF THE NATURE OF NEW COMMUNITIES

Having examined some examples of squatter communities and their role in the developing city it is now possible to consider them in relation to the theme of the development of new communities and how they aid our understanding of the central processes involved.

The squatter communities demonstrate the necessity in new community formation for there to be in existence a common system of values and goals shared by those intending to create the new community. It was from this basis of agreement amongst the urban dwellers that the organisation emerged which enabled the squatting to be successful. The importance of organisation of the community both before and after its physical foundation also emerges as important to the eventual success and secure establishment of the community. It was because the invasion at Cuevas was a well-organised one of a large number of families, that although the authorities attempted to dislodge them, they proved unsuccessful and eventually recognised the community as a permanent fixture. This could not have happened without the careful planning, swift occupation and allocation of plots covering the area decided upon by the founding organisation. This organisation, then, became the association which continued to regulate the affairs of the community. Another important factor in the early development was the existence of conflict with the authorities which reinforced the sense of solidarity amongst the members of the community. This and the subsequent decline in popular involvement in the running of the community as it became a recognised entity and normal relationships became established between the squatter colony and the city is reminiscent of the 'phase hypothesis' discussed earlier of community development in which it was found on British housing estates, that community orientation declined as the area became settled and the initial problems and difficulties became satisfactorily resolved. Finally there was the existence of selective migration to the squatter colonies with some form of control over new residents which enabled the preservation of the identity of the community.

The other aspect of the process of community formation which the squatter communities illustrate is the relationship between the 'planners' and the 'planned for'. This is in this case a source of continuing value conflict as the demands of the squatters and the solutions they have adopted conflict with those of the official planning norms. They also present an acute problem to the planners. Should they, for example, be removed from the cities as essentially areas of below-standard housing with attendant risks to the health and 'good' development of the city? Or should they be improved so that a partnership can be established between the government planners and the people who live in the communities? This has been attempted in some of the South American cities, e.g. Rio with its grants to the *favela* associations.[40] This policy of improvement, however, can have the effect of creating yet further squatting as a means of obtaining a shelter in a continuing overcrowded city either in entirely new areas or in the existing areas. If the latter, then by increasing densities this may provide a stimulus to some of the original squatters to seek further enhancement of their position by moving outwards thus creating new communities. This would bring about a similar kind of city spread to that which has occurred in the developed cities through private speculation and building and rising social aspirations which have been transferred into obtaining single family housing in a suburban or fringe setting rather than within the central city areas. The future of squatter communities is also likely

114 The Quest for Community

to be affected by their growing size in relation to the city population as a whole. In some they already constitute at least half the city population and if present trends continue, as appears likely, they will soon become a majority of the population within many developing cities. This will no doubt have a considerable effect upon its political decision-making as local governments will be dependent upon the votes and support of the squatters. This political influence may well lead to the development of a much more adaptive approach to the new communities whereby squatter associations and government work together to bring about collective social development and concrete physical improvements within the communities.

Chapter 6

Ideological Communities

The types of new developments examined so far have all been within the compass of the prevailing value system of the societies concerned. They have not represented attempts either to create an alternative system of societal organisation reflecting different social values or attempts to preserve an older value system and societal organisation. The creation of new towns, as we have seen from a previous chapter, was an attempt to create a 'community' which exemplified current planning and social ideology regarding the ideal spatial and social arrangements of populations. The conflict which lay at the heart of such developments was in the divergence between the values of the creators and those of the residents who often aspired to more individualistic expressions of the current social ideology. The area of 'intentional' or 'utopian' communities is, therefore, important, as it provides insight into the way in which alternative community value systems have been created and preserved. The problems, conflicts and tensions which have characterised these experiments also provide valuable insight into the nature of community structure and efficacy of different types of social organisation.

The communitarian movement has a long and interesting history of development, tracing its origin back to early pre-Christian religious sects like the Essenes.[1] This Hebrew sect was characterised by a distinctive philosophy, joint ownership of property, control of private assets and collective consumption. The communal movement up to the nineteenth century was dominated by religious communes, tracing their inspiration back to the early Christian communes. These early communes were replaced from around the fourth century by monastic orders who were originally rural based but also appeared within towns and cities from the twelfth century. In the nineteenth century there was the development of sectarian communes with the spread of socialist and co-operative doctrines, stemming from, on the one hand St Simon, Owen and Fourier and, on the other hand groups like the Rochdale Pioneers. The communal societies which have arisen have consequently diverse origins. Some have originated in a belief in primitive communism which found its inspiration in the activities of the New Testament Christians; others in social disturbances and the new idealism associated with them, for example the French Revolution and growth of socialism; yet others were the product of the migration of settlers into new countries, particularly the movement to America in the eighteenth and nineteenth centuries, this movement being largely stimulated by hostility and threats to the existence of the groups in their country of origin. The need for collective security to withstand hostilities of one sort and another has also been a feature of many new communities, for example in the development of the kibbutz in Israel. In order to look more closely at the nature of such communities a number will be examined in greater detail: the Hutterite Brethren, as an example of a religious-based communal society which is constantly creating new communities; New Harmony, as an example of the Owenite socialist phase of communal development; and finally the kibbutz and other contemporary communal development.

I   HUTTERITE BRETHREN

The Hutterite communities are now found in North Dakota in the United States and principally in Alberta and Saskatchewan in Canada.[2] The Hutterites, however, originated in Austria in the sixteenth century as an Anabaptist sect. The principles which are still at the centre of the present life of the communities have remained virtually unchanged since they were first formulated in the sixteenth century. The current communities still reflect the original pattern of social organisation developed by one of the founders of the sect, Jacob Hutter. The bases of the original communities were the community of goods, pacifism, adult baptism and exclusiveness. These particular characteristics led the communities into repeated conflicts with orthodox religion, both Protestant and Catholic, and the repeated persecution of the sect. The Hutterites also attracted hostility from the state and economic interests, due to the generally efficient nature of their communities' agricultural and craft industries which made them prosperous. The early period of their development from 1565 to 1592, which was spent in Moravia, to which they migrated as a consequence of persecution in Austria, was one of stability and prosperity and this period is now looked upon as the 'golden age' of Hutterite development. However, in the seventeenth century, persecution caught up with them and drove them out of Moravia. This migration split the band of Hutterites into two, one moving into Slovakia and the other into Transylvania. The next one hundred or so years saw a steady decline in the number of Hutterites through the various attacks on their beliefs and way of life. By 1760 the group which had moved into Hungary were virtually extinct but the Transylvanian group fared rather better and began, in the latter half of the eighteenth century, to re-establish its communitarian principles. Once more, however, they were forced to migrate, this time to Russia where they lived and prospered for about a hundred years, finally ending up in the Crimea region in the 1840s. In 1870, however, the Russian Government withdrew the privileges they had enjoyed, particularly that of military exemption and so the Hutterites once more migrated in 1874 to North America settling initially in North and South Dakota. The original communities established in 1874 in America contained 800 Hutterites and it is from the three original communities that the current Hutterite population has grown. The Hutterites are divided into three *leutes* named after the leaders of the first three North American communities. In 1965 the number of Hutterites in the various communities had grown to 17,800. Of these, 12,500 were in Canada and 5,300 were in the United States. This population was contained within 164 colonies.

The basis of the social system of the Hutterite communities is to be found in their religious beliefs which include the belief in self-help and, so, the avoidance or minimisation of contact in and involvement with the world. This has led to the communities being physically isolated from the surrounding settlements and society. They also believe that the perfect society can be established now if the correct principles are employed. These deny personal, individual accumulation of wealth and allow communal holding of property and wealth in the manner of the early Christian disciples.

The main elements of the social organisation of the communities demonstrate the integral importance of their religious values. The organisation of community life is under the direction of a council of elders, elected by the assembly of the baptised, adult, male members of the community. This council consists of the Head Preacher, who is the supreme authority, the Assistant Preacher, the Householder, the Farm Boss and the German schoolteacher. The Head Preacher, as the religious leader, is responsible for the overall well-being of the community and is the one responsible for the teaching of the Hutterite tradition and for its maintainance within the community. This tradition, which is mostly written, takes the form of books, sermons and hymns, many of which date from the sixteenth-century original Hutterite communities. Many of the hymns relate to periods of persecution when they were used to maintain the spirits of the faithful whilst they were in prison. This tradition is still written in its original German, which is also the language of the community and its religious activities, i.e. its services. The role of the Preacher is not as an interpreter of the tradition in the sense that he relates it to current situations; it is rather as a repeater and guardian of the tradition that the Preacher functions. The German schoolteacher is the other important member concerned with the telling of the Hutterite tradition and it is within the German School that the children learn the values of the community. The council of elders is responsible to the assembly which discusses and approves policy and elects the various position holders within the community.³

The communities are based upon agricultural production and this side of activities is the responsibility of the Farm Boss. The communities operate a system of large-scale mixed farming and have, on the whole, been very successful, being able to hold large acreages and to utilise them efficiently. The agricultural production within the communities makes use of technological advances and modern methods of husbandry, cropping, etc., as long as these are seen to be useful to the agricultural productivity within the community. The self-sufficiency of the communities extends beyond agricultural activity to the creation of their own workshops for repair and maintainance and even construction of farm and colony equipment, like furniture. They also have domestic production in the form of clothing, shoemaking, etc. There is role differentiation to be found within the communities with the men being principally involved in agricultural activities whereas the women are more concerned with the domestic work of the communities, such as the cooking, cleaning, painting of the houses, making of the clothes, etc. There are status distinctions between the sexes, with the women having no formal rights within the elective procedures of the communities. They very probably have considerable informal influence upon activities but this has to be done via their husbands or other males, rather than directly via the assembly. In addition to the Farm Boss, the Householder has the responsibility for the economic prosperity of the colony, controlling its budget and ensuring that capital is accumulated for the community 'branching', i.e. foundation of daughter communities. In addition to these major office holders there are, under the Farm Boss, a number of Farm Enterprise Managers, the exact number depending on the range of farm activities practised within any particular community. The final level is that of the labourers. This group consists of all men over fifteen years, not in managerial positions.

The organisation and economic activities are geared to the production of surpluses which are accumulated to provide the necessary capital to buy land and equipment to set up a daughter community when branching occurs.[4] The process of branching is essential for the vitality of the communities and occurs usually after at least fifteen years of community life. There are a number of reasons for this division process. First, there are limitations on the size of the population that can be supported on a given acreage of land entirely dependent upon an agricultural base. The Hutterites believe that the maximum number that can be contained in a community is about 150 therefore as the community approaches this level it divides into two. The division is carried out by the male heads of the families by lot so that a balanced population is achieved in terms of age and sex composition. The new colony is seen as a 'daughter' colony and, until it is fully established, receives help and support from the 'mother' colony. The success of the new community is aided by the fact that it is established as a farm prior to the arrival of a permanent population. Secondly, division is necessary because of the high rates of fertility amongst the Hutterites, to whom birth control practices are forbidden.[5] Without branching the standard of living would fall due to the larger numbers having to acquire a livelihood from limited agricultural output. If there was no branching the only alternative way of maintaining or increasing living standards would be to introduce alternative bases of activity, to include industrial as well as agricultural activities. This the Hutterites have no wish to do. Thirdly, there is the belief that small communities both work better and are easier to control and organise. The fourth reason is that, as the communities get larger, there is a greater possibility of cliques being established, which tend to monopolise the managerial positions and consequently prevent the younger members from having an opportunity to acquire a managerial position. This situation of blocked opportunities is likely to cause frustration amongst younger members. With branching at regular intervals, new positions are created and vacancies are left in the 'mother' community. Branching is thus functional for the stability of the community.

The Hutterites are, for the most part, divided along age and sex lines.[6] This has already become apparent in the division between the sexes with regard to work and participation in the formal decision-making procedures. There are a number of distinct age groupings through which the individual passes. These are 'house children' up to the age of two years, when the child spends his time with his mother; kindergarten up to five years; school from five to fourteen years, which includes both the German school from which the child learns Hutterite history and culture and the English school where he is taught by a non-Hutterite teacher the approved curriculum of the particular state in which the community is situated. After fifteen, the young person enters the work force and is usually given hard and exacting tasks. The next significant stage for the male is baptism which normally takes place around twenty and this marks the entry into the full adult community and confers on him the right to participate in community decision-making. The last stage is the passing out of this group through marriage which usually occurs in the mid twenties. Marriage within the Hutterite community is endogamous and patrilocality is practised. The marriages are normally kept within a particular *leute* and through marriage, relationships are established and strengthened between the various communities within the *leute*. This particular form of marriage, particularly its patrilocality, means that the most important informal grouping is that of male siblings as they, alone, have a lifetime solidarity. The children are not completely separated from their parents but from three onwards spend their day in the nursery and school systems, eating together and spending their time with their peers and the German teacher. Family relationships are, however, important and the children live with their parents.

Having looked at some of the main aspects of social organisation, it is now necessary to consider what factors have contributed to their stability and continuity since the sixteenth century as communal organisations.[7] There are several reasons which can be advanced. The first of these is the religious ideology of the group and the way in which the pattern of life has remained virtually unchanged since the inception of the communities. This is because of their separatist existence which has isolated them from the changes taking place in the wider society. This separatism is associated with agricultural activities in rural settings thus leading to a physical isolation. Linked with this ideology is the system of socialisation of the children with the community controlling the education within the German School and its insistence that the English school should be within the community therefore within the influence of the elders who would be able to ensure that the teaching was not at odds with their beliefs. The English school is seen essentially as the place where techniques like arithmetic and English are learned rather than the place where education is received, this being provided by the German School. A further factor lies in the efficiency of the economic and social organisation of the communities via their division of labour and specialisation of tasks. This enables both the current needs of all the members to be met, thus relieving them of financial anxieties regarding the care and bringing up of their children and the care of the sick and old, and the accumulation of capital for eventual branching. The existence of democratic decision-making processes allows all the adult male members of the community to be involved in policy-making and planning, although there does exist an authoritarian element in the organisation via the inviolability of the tradition and religious truth which is associated with the Head Preacher. Changes, however, do occur in the rules of the community through what Eaton has termed a process of 'controlled acculturation',[8] whereby the Hutterites accept practices from American culture and integrate them into their existing system. The process occurs when pressures for change become strong enough to threaten the harmony and stability of the group. In these circumstances the rule under pressure ceases to be enforced and, at a later stage, the rule is recast to give formal recognition and therefore control over the new practice. By this means change can be contained within the framework of Hutterite culture. Another factor is that the Hutterites appear to have produced a workable balance between family autonomy in the provision of housing and activities and communal living in terms of the children's collective education. Further, there has been very little addition of new members from outside the communities, consequently, all share the common socialisation experience and there is little problem regarding the integration of newcomers. The intermarriage within the communities provides additional links which tie the individuals into the Hutterite system.

The last area to be considered is that of the problems and tensions found in these communities. These come from two sources, external to the community and internal. The external are produced by the contacts which the Hutterites have with the much more individualistic values common within contemporary American society. Their external contacts also bring them into contact with an affluent consumption oriented society which contrasts markedly with the principles of austerity and the rejection of personal accumulation of possessions which lies at the heart of their culture. Other external pressures which have brought problems for the communities have been wars which have caused tension between the pacifist Hutterites who were unwilling to enter the armed forces and the governments and local communities of the countries within which they lived. This particular kind of pressure was one of the principle causes of their migration from the United States to Canada. Another external problem has been the imposition of land restrictions which have prevented the communities operating their branching policies as freely as they would have liked, having the effect of increasing the distances between the 'mother' and 'daughter' colonies from the ideal distance of twenty to thirty miles to distances of over one hundred miles. Restrictions on land purchases were also responsible for the movement of Hutterites into Saskatchewan from Alberta.[9] Finally there has been a certain amount of tension associated with the role of the public education provided by the English school where the syllabus is controlled by the outside education authorities.

Internal tensions arise from leadership failures due to the fairly centralised organisation. Much of the success of the community is due to the managerial competence of its elders. Failures, therefore, within communities are often attributed to the leaders and occasionally these have to be replaced by the *leute*, which operates in a supporting fashion for its member colonies. Finally the loss of members from the communities has an effect upon their morale. The number of members who have left permanently is, however, very small so that losses of this type are not at the present a serious threat to the stability and cohesiveness of the communities.

The Hutterite communities represent an interesting type of communal organisation which has been reproducing itself for over four hundred years. Its unity lies in its basis in religious values which are accepted by all the members of the community, in its efficient patterns of social and economic organisation, and in its closed nature as a society which is produced by its physical isolation as a rural agricultural community, its endogamous marriages and its self-sufficient economy.

II   OWENITE SOCIALIST COMMUNITY—NEW HARMONY

The second example is drawn from the nineteenth-century experience of the Owenite socialist experiments in communal organisation in the United States of which there were seven altogether with New Harmony being the first and best known.[10] New Harmony, in contrast to the long history of the Hutterites, only lasted for two years. Owen, the founder, believed that to change men what was necessary was a new physical and social environment in which they could live and work. He believed that this environment could best be provided in the small community in which communal ownership of property was practised.[11] Owen began his experiments in Britain with his venture of creating a new physical environment for the workers at New Lanark. This, however, did not involve communal ownership, the workers still being employed in the normal manner in the factory. Owen, however, found the opportunity in the United States in 1825 to try a more far-reaching experiment in communal living when the former Rappite community of Harmony came up for sale. Owen bought up the land and buildings of this community in 1825 and announced his intention of setting up a communal society to be called New Harmony. In response to this announcement eight hundred assorted individuals moved to New Harmony. The history of this community is a somewhat chequered one from the beginning, because Owen had not clearly worked out how his principles of communal living should be put into practice. His speeches and writings were at a theoretical level rather than at a practical organisational level of a real community with real people. The original settlers were attracted to the community for a large variety of reasons; some, mostly the middle-class intellectuals, because they shared, or thought they did, Owen's ideals and philosophy; others, perhaps the majority, came because of Owen's reputation as a generous philanthropist and hoped that he would support them without their having to work particularly hard.

In 1825 when New Harmony was inaugurated, the preliminary society was established which lasted for the first seven months until Owen himself arrived.[12] During this early period the community was governed by an elected committee but real control lay in the hands of one of Owen's sons. The community suffered overcrowding from the beginning due to admitting too many people. It also suffered because of the composition of the population which lacked craftsmen able to operate the machinery taken over from the Rappites in the purchase of the community. Consequently neither productive nor agricultural activity was begun for a considerable period of time and when it did commence most production was solely for internal consumption. This meant that the community was dependent for its survival on Owen's money.

The arrival of Owen, after the first seven months, marked the ending of the preliminary society and the establishment of New Harmony proper into which all the existing residents were automatically admitted. The first constitution soon foundered as did the society and both were reorganised into a system of three independent communities, the School or Educational Society, the Agricultural Society and the Mechanic Society. These three societies were linked together into a federation by a Board of Union which was to arrange trading between the three societies. This scheme, however, like the first, soon became bogged down in conflicts between the three societies and the cessation of trade and support for the School Society by the other two. This led to yet another reorganisation in which it was proposed to dissolve the existing societies and reform them once more as a centralised unit. This once more failed to work and again it was proposed to decentralise with a central community based upon the village of New Harmony to be surrounded by a number of linked communities. None of these, however, became established and finally the whole experiment ended in 1827 after only two years of existence.

Having outlined briefly the history of New Harmony it is now necessary to examine the reasons for its short and disturbed life and its ultimate failure. The first reason lies in the problems of organisation and structure. The Hutterites had a clearly defined system of hierarchical elected officials in charge of different sectors of life and it was noted that, given good leadership, this worked well. In New Harmony both of these appeared to have been lacking. Owen was not a good administrator of the community nor did he, via the various constitutions that he devised, establish a good organisation. The second problem was that the community was subject to a number of ideological controversies between Owen and others which affected the unity of the community. The most far-reaching was between Owen and Maclure which led to the separation of the School Society from the rest of New Harmony and a legal dispute between Owen and Maclure in 1827.[13] Thirdly, there was the lack of a cohesive ideological force or set of identities amongst the members. The entry was unrestricted therefore the original settlers held diverse aspirations, some shared those of Owen, others were communitarians of differing and in some cases more extreme views than those of Owen regarding the extent of private ownership allowable, others had no real ideological commitment to communal living and were quite happy to live off Owen's generosity. The failure here to provide a means of examining the candidates for membership of the community, a process found within most other communal societies, proved very costly to the health and vitality of the society. The diversity and conflicts between the various factions led in fact to many of those originally sympathetic to Owen's views becoming disillusioned and leaving the community. The low morale is illustrated by the steady progression of people away from the community during its lifetime. Fourthly, Owen failed to resolve the basic question of the nature of the system of property rights and communal ownership that he intended to be adopted. For the lifetime of New Harmony, Owen remained the landlord, owning the land and equipment himself. This led to charges that he was not in fact a communitarian at all.

The New Harmony community gives valuable evidence as to the basic requirements of communal organisation. These are a set of shared values and beliefs, selection of the participants and the existence of a means of expelling or sanctioning members to bring about conformity to the values of the society and to prevent the inter-personal conflicts, characteristic of New Harmony, from dominating and disrupting life. Also necessary is the existence of a form of social organisation which expresses in its structure these values, i.e. has communal ownership of property and practises communal consumption. It is further essential that the organisation provides and maintains an effective economic base to make the community viable.

III KIBBUTZIM

The kibbutz finds its origin and ideology in necessity. The ideal of the kibbutz as a 'fellowship of all who share a common faith' existed before the establishment of the first kibbutz and was a product of the European Jewish youth movements of the early part of the twentieth century.[14] The kibbutz, hence, was organised and founded to express a given set of social values. There were, however, other influences upon their establishment. One which was important was physical security. Another was the need to provide a vehicle of transition for the immigrant population, many of whom had no previous knowledge of agricultural work. The kibbutz movement with its central theme of the importance of productive labour, in the context of the development of Israel, filled a pioneering role in the creation of a class of Israeli productive workers who secured the frontiers and practised self-help, not relying upon Arab labour.

The kibbutzim have developed since the first at Degania in 1910 into three separate federations which have divided along both ideological and organisational lines, with varying degrees of commitment to left-wing political groups and with differences in size and composition of activities between agricultural and industrial production. There have also developed differences between the federations in their attitudes towards collective living, particularly consumption and settlement size. The kibbutzim were founded on and continue to be organised in accord with a belief in co-operative living which means that all property is owned collectively, all work is collectively organised and so also is living. The underlying values of the kibbutz society have been identified as four in number. These are, first, that physically productive labour has the highest prestige and value, this arises in part as a reaction to the kind of work done by Jews prior to migration, mostly in service occupations, and partly in response to the needs of the new nation. Secondly, and allied to the first, is the belief in self-sufficiency, with all the jobs within the community being done by the members, without the use of outside paid labour. Thirdly, property used and produced by the community belongs to the entire community. Fourthly, there is complete equality within the community.

This kind of communal society is organised in many ways

similarly to that of the Hutterites, but with important distinctions. The structure of the kibbutz has three units each concerned with one aspect of its activities, the economic, the social and ideological, and the educational.[15] The principle economic activity within the kibbutz is agriculture, with the development of modern, highly sophisticated mixed farming. There has also been the development in more recent years of kibbutz industry to provide the necessary wealth to support the continued growth of the kibbutz population. Figures, for example, drawn from one of the federations show that although the basic economic activity is still agriculture, industrial activity has been increasing, e.g. between 1962–6 industrial activity rose as a proportion of total economic activity from 15 to 17 per cent. Alternatively the same source shows that 82 per cent of the kibbutz population are resident in a kibbutz which has some industry. The role of industry within the kibbutz is a contentious one and is sometimes given as a reason for the 'crisis' within the kibbutz movement. The second unit, the social and ideological, is concerned with the relations between the kibbutz and its federation. There is a requirement upon each kibbutz to provide a certain number of its members to work for a time for the national federation either in Israel or abroad. The kibbutzim have been very much political communities, this varying somewhat with the particular federation, but they have all conceived of themselves as pioneering a new way of life which would lead to the reconstruction of society as a whole along socialist co-operative lines. The final unit of organisation is the educational which is concerned with the task of ensuring the continuity of kibbutz values. The educational system was established on communitarian lines to free the woman from her ties and responsibility of bringing up her children so that she could participate equally within the life of the community and also to prepare the coming generation for communal life. The system is organised in five stages with the new babies entering the infants' house where they stay until one year old, when they transfer to the toddlers' house, thence to kindergarten, primary and finally high school.[16] In this latter school part of the time is spent in working in some aspect of the economy. On completion of school, the entry of the young person into the kibbutz is not automatic but is on the basis of election by the kibbutz meeting.

The kibbutz meeting, which is made up of all the full members of the kibbutz, both male and female, is the main decision-making body and decisions are taken on the basis of majority voting. The actual organisation of the various activities is undertaken by elected committees and a secretariat of central officers. These are the Farm Manager, who is in charge of the agricultural production of the kibbutz, the Secretary, Treasurer and work organiser, who is in charge of allocating the members of the particular branches of activity. These central positions are elected by the general meeting and the holders do not have any special privileges awarded to them, although prestige does accrue by the nature of the responsibilities that are associated with the positions. Various committees cover the whole range of activities of the kibbutz and are places within which activities and policies are considered, hence they provide an opportunity for the members to be involved in policy formation and decision-making.[17]

The other important features of the kibbutz are first the principle of equality which governs the distribution of resources, according to need and provides, therefore, for all regardless of their current contribution to the work of the kibbutz, i.e. the old, the sick and nursing mothers. The second important feature is collective consumption of food, housing and clothing. Food is provided for all in the communal dining-room which also serves as the venue for the general meeting. This used to be the hub of the social life of the kibbutz. Living quarters are provided according to uniform standards and during the early years these were extremely spartan but have improved with the increases in wealth of the communities. Clothing was originally made to a standard pattern within the dressmaking and tailoring shops and each member received an issue of clothing every year. This standard provision has been modified, in recent years, to permit greater expression of personal choice. The most radical departure here has been in those kibbutzim which have allowed the issue of money for the purchase of clothing in the form of an annual allowance. This is seen by many of the kibbutzim as a dangerous move away from the principles of collective living.

According to some observers of the kibbutz, there has developed a 'crisis' which is the product of both internal and external strains. It is valuable to examine these to see what light they shed upon the resilience of communal organisations to accommodate or withstand pressure. These strains can be examined under five broad headings. First, there are those related to problems of consumption.[18] The accepted view of collective consumption involves allocation to the members on the basis of need and does not permit individual variety or supplementation. Also the level of consumption has been kept at a relatively low level, lower than that common in the rest of Israel, as priority within the kibbutz has been given to production. The formulation of the consumption budget is a source of far greater controversy and friction than is the establishment of the production targets and budget. This is because this area impinges much more upon the way individuals live their lives and to individual aspirations for greater freedom of choice as to clothing, food and personal possessions. In this area most of the kibbutzim have made concessions in the direction of allowing greater freedom of choice, but the more this is allowed, the more it conflicts with the basic values of the kibbutz ideology.

The second area of conflict between the kibbutz ideology and its members is in the realm of interpersonal behaviour.[19] This has a number of aspects. The first is the decline noted by observers in the importance of group experience for the members of the kibbutz. In the early days the common dining-room was the centre of the kibbutz life, with the members staying together in the evenings for the community meetings to discuss both internal and external policies. The current trend, however, is away from the common dining-room as the centre of activities to the family and to the small group who meet in their own rooms. This change is attributable to such things as the lessening of the pioneering role of the members as the community prospers and this lessens the sense of collective consciousness. The tendency towards a small group of intimate friends as the focus of an individual's life is seen also to be a function of ageing which leads to a greater stress upon privacy and individual experience. There is also the conflict which has always existed between the family and the community which is highlighted by the questions surrounding the policy of separating the children from their parents through the system of collective education. Here again modification has been introduced to allow parents, particularly mothers, a greater amount of interaction and involvement with their children. In one of the kibbutz federations there has been the provision for children now to sleep in their parents' quarters. This conflict between involvement in community as against familial roles is most acute in the women and at the centre of much of the discontent lies the problematic position of women.[20] Kibbutz ideology gives to a woman an equal place but in practice this goal is not fully achieved. The highest status work because of the ideology is productive work. Partly as a result of their child-bearing role and also due to the often hard nature of the physical work, the majority of women are involved in non-productive work. The principle work of the women is in the domestic side of kibbutz life, cooking, cleaning, making clothes, working in the kindergarten, etc. This means they are performing very much the same kind of work that a woman would do as a wife and mother in a conventional family setting. However, here because of the collective system of child rearing and education, her domestic work is not complemented by the satisfactions obtained from normal familial roles. This means that many of the women are dissatisfied with their position as it is one which brings them little intrinsic satisfaction. Hence, their pressure to modify the system to allow greater control for the mother over her children and to allow improvements in the level of domestic comfort.

The third area that gives evidence of strains is the number of people who are leaving the kibbutzim. The figures here indicate that the numbers leaving over the period from 1949 to 1965 have varied from 9·7 per cent in 1949 to 3·1 per cent in 1965.[21] This has not been a steady decline but one which has shown a number of variations. The figures fell until 1956 when they reached 3·7 per cent, they then rose again to 6 per cent by the late 1950s and then declined again to 3·1 per cent. A possible explanation for these variations could be that they reflect the external pressures upon Israel, e.g. the low figure for 1956 coincides with the Suez crisis. Also, the increased buoyancy of the Israeli economy during the periods of relative calm would create attractive vacancies outside the kibbutz. This figure of total leavers is perhaps not as important as that for young leavers, those who were brought up in the kibbutz and then rather than entering the kibbutz, decided to leave. Here the figure has varied between 5 and 8 per cent per annum depending upon which federation is being examined.[22] This shows a sizeable proportion are rejecting the values of the community.

Another indicator of the overall vitality of the community is the ease with which the responsible positions of Farm Manager, Secretary and Treasurer are filled. Here there is evidence of increasing difficulty in fulfilling these responsible positions. Does this mean that the commitment to the kibbutz has weakened, hence a different type of motivation will be needed in future for position holders? If so, then the communities would be moving away from their original form as collective societies based upon an undifferentiated structure and equalitarian ideology.

The fifth area of tensions has arisen over the role of paid labour which undermines the principles of self-sufficiency. The kibbutz, however, have suffered from labour shortages, particularly those which have departed from a purely agricultural base. The proportion of hired labour, for example, within kibbutz industry as a whole was 59 per cent in 1966. The need for labour and the expansion of industry to provide the higher standard of living now demanded by the members of the kibbutz opens the danger of the communities becoming differentiated into two classes, through the emergence of a wage labour class. This represents both a denial of the kibbutz ideology of equality and also the introduction of a group into the kibbutz who do not share the values of the community.

Lastly, there are the changed external conditions of Israeli society. The kibbutzim were part of the pioneering movement which enabled the state of Israel to be found by providing an agricultural base and securing the outlying frontier areas. As the state has developed there has been a shift away from the importance of such agricultural communities and an emphasis upon industrial development, and the importance of individual incentives and achievements. With the stabilisation of the state the climate of opinion has changed and so the kibbutzim have tended to decline in importance in both functions and ideological inspiration for the society as a whole. Leon, writing on the kibbutz, claims that 'the cult of the state, the denigration of voluntary social forces and the process of capital normalisation have thrown into relief the contradictions between the kibbutz and its environment'.[23] Despite this changed relationship, the kibbutz still plays a part in shaping the political life of the nation with, for example, a disproportionately high number of members of parliament from the kibbutzim. They have also provided the scene for much of the music and artistic work of contemporary Israeli society. Nevertheless, the changed attitudes of the wider society to the members of the kibbutzim, which no longer sees them as the pioneers and leaders of society, does cause both problems of adjustment to their new role and also a re-examination of their purpose both ideologically, as vanguards of a new society and as collective communities, in particular in relation to their standard of living and the organisation of their work.

To set against these problems and pressures upon the communal society there are also unifying forces. These have been identified as first, the social and material equality which is practised and the way in which the society provides for all the needs of its members. Secondly, the consciousness of moral superiority which arises from the ideological basis of the kibbutz and the value placed upon productive manual labour. Thirdly, there exists a high degree of identification with the culture of the kibbutz which is a product of the socialisation whereby from an early age the child is educated in a collective manner to appreciate the values of a communal society.[24] Fourthly, Spiro, from his study of the kibbutz, points to the way the kibbutz operates as an extended family, providing mutual supports of various kinds bound together by an ideology which functions like a religion, to give form, coherence and purpose to the communities. The basis of these various reinforcing processes is the way in which the common ideology operates to provide the basis of shared meanings which unite the people together in a collective community. The community is voluntary and selection is not automatic, consequently those who do not share the values of the community are not included, hence the conflicts and tensions operate within a framework of broad agreement as to the character and ultimate goals of the communal society.

IV CONTEMPORARY COMMUNES

A further type of ideologically based community is the commune, represented by small groups of individuals who join together to practise collective living in one form or another. This particular type of community has shown signs of increasing in recent years in Western industrial societies. These communes are seen to have developed in 'response to and part of a profound revolution to transform society'.[25] They have emerged out of a rejection of the existing dominant social values emphasising individualism and have been an attempt to create alternative societies based upon communal living and a return to a simpler pattern of life.[26] There are different strands to this movement in Britain. First, the Commune Movement, which has gathered together a number of groups and acts as a co-ordinating and advisory body, which publishes its own journal. Secondly, the 'Digger' movement and finally, religious movements, both Christian and non-Christian.

The Commune Movement arose out of the merging of three separate groups which all began in the early 1960s. These were the Vegan community, the Agricultural and Land Industries Mutual Support Association and Community Experiments Unlimited. All these small groups were concerned with escaping from the 'dominance of Man by Machine in favour of a simpler life'. The means of achieving this aim were to be found in the establishment of usually agrarian based, self-sufficient communities using organic farming. These various groups came together in 1968 with the establishment of the Commune Movement as a distinct organisation. The objects of this movement were stated as to create 'a federal society of communities wherein everyone shall be free to do whatever he wishes provided only that he does not transgress the freedom of another'.[27] Since its inception the membership has grown to 300 in 1971 and 427 in 1972 (December) and the circulation of its journal to around 2,200.[28] Although the movement has grown in numbers, the actual number of communes created has been small and of relatively short duration.

The second strand is that of the Diggers who owe their origin to the seventeenth-century group of rural peasants who established three small rural communes, during the Commonwealth, but whose aims were too extreme for Cromwell and who suffered at his hand.[29] The movement reappeared in its contemporary form in the 1960s in San Francisco and the British Diggers were founded in 1967. Since then the Diggers have established a commune on the island of Dorinish, off the west coast of Ireland in 1969.

The third group are the religious-based communities. These share with the first two groups the belief in the value of communal living. In the Christian communes, this has been associated with a return to the 'primitive Christianity' of the early disciples, together with the provision of a 'therapeutic community' in which people might find 'love, healing and prayer' and then return to the wider society.[30] In a similar vein, the communes dedicated to meditation, strongly influenced by Eastern religions, are also seen as therapeutic communities in which people may withdraw from the world to come to a realisation of themselves.

Having looked at something of the variety of origins of contemporary communes, it is necessary to look at their structure, stability and organisation. Evidence on communes in Britain is at present sketchy but what there is suggests that they are small in size with the majority having less than ten members. The precise number of communes is difficult to estimate and appears to vary from year to year due to the relatively short length of time that many of the communes are in existence. In the Commune Movement Directory for 1970 there were listed 37 secular communes and a further 12 being projected.[31] In the most recent directory (1972), however, the number has fallen to 24. Of these 24, only 15 were listed in 1970. Hence of the 37 which existed in 1970 over half appear to have been disbanded.[32] Of those listed in both the 1970 and 1972 directories, the majority of the communes had been in existence for less than five years. In a recent study of Christian communes the author lists 26 Christian communes which have been formed since 1960.[33] In both cases the majority of the members of the communes are from the younger age groups, predominantly the under 30s.

The organisation within the communes varies considerably from those where there is complete communal ownership of property and sharing of all goods and activities, to ones where there is still a high degree of individual separateness with a system of common contributions into a central fund to pay the rent, etc. Similarly there is variation on the extent to which entry to the communes is controlled and a common ideology exists. The lack of clearly held aims and common values has led to much instability amongst the communes with quite frequent splits and divisions between the members leading either to the breaking up of the communes or the splitting off of part of the original group of members. The growth of communes does not appear to have been associated with the growth of a common binding ideology which they all share, rather it has been characterised by considerable variations between the various communes in their aims, size and organisation.

This final group of ideological communities shows that attempts to create alternative societies with differing value systems are occurring in both religious and non-religious spheres particularly among the younger sections of the population. However, there is no one dominating alternative pattern which is developing, rather the picture is one of relative instability and short duration. This is less pronounced among the religious communes as they have a more clearly defined aim and purpose.

V CONCLUSIONS

The examination of different communities has revealed a number of common processes and important differences which help to clarify the nature of such communities and in particular the reasons for their continued existence.

The communities were all created with some kind of ideological base, either religious or sectarian, although Spiro has claimed that the kibbutzim too are 'religious in character'. In all cases it is the ideology which gives coherence and structure of the communities. The cases of New Harmony and some of the contemporary communes clearly show that where the ideological base is not accepted or is open to wide divergences of interpretation without some kind of official doctrine which has majority approval, the community quickly founders. Secondly, they demonstrate the necessity for good organisation which allows the society to operate efficiently hence providing the necessary standard of living. Both the Hutterites and the kibbutzim have developed efficient, technologically advanced agricultural operations and the kibbutz has complemented this with industry. In New Harmony the organisation was poor and the community never became financially viable, it was always dependent upon Owen's money. A basic difference emerges here between the Hutterites and the kibbutzim in that the former are entirely agricultural which means they have to operate a system of branching in order to maintain their level of living. The kibbutzim, in contrast, have had no limits on population and have, therefore, been more and more forced to find alternative sources of income to agricultural to maintain their economic viability and to improve their standard of living in response to members' desires. Thirdly, both the Hutterites and the kibbutzim operate a 'rite-de-passage' to achieve full membership which operates as a selective mechanism which means that entry to full membership requires a positive decision both by the individual and by the whole community. New Harmony and some of the contemporary communes again in contrast operated no selection procedures and, therefore, acquired more highly diversified populations with little in common. Fourthly, the importance in all the collective communities of the socialisation process with its emphasis upon communal values and minimisation of parental control over the educational process, and the acceptance by the community of control over both teachers, pupils and content of the education given. Finally, the majority of the communities operated within a defined locality and the world of the communities was conducted almost entirely within this locality. This enabled a degree of physical and social isolation to be practised which helped to emphasise their separate identity. The importance of the common work and living base for the community is shown by the unsuccessful attempts at developing urban kibbutzim. For example one at Efal, a suburb of Tel Aviv which was begun in 1947.[34] Here the members lived together and pooled their earnings which were obtained in jobs in the city as a whole. Difficulties here developed quite soon over the distribution of earnings and the subsidisation by the higher earners of the others. In such a situation the conflict of values and contrasts between the kibbutzim and the remainder of the city are much more acute than between the relatively isolated agricultural kibbutzim and Israel urban society with its sharply contrasting classes.

The communal societies examined here also demonstrate common problems which are already familiar as they occur in other community situations that have been examined, particularly in the new towns. The basic problem in all cases is that of the conflict between the individual and the community, between personal values and desires and those of collective ideology. This is well illustrated by the problem of collective consumption where the allocation of each according to need, which is the ideological principle, causes controversy as it denies the opportunity for individual choice and the expression of individual taste in such things as clothing and furnishing of homes. This basic problem is never solved in a communal society, it is simply accommodated and is consequently always a source of tension, one which can usually be managed. When it fails to be managed, however, then the society begins to disintegrate as the allegiances to the collective ideology which give overall shape to the community become attenuated. Here the history of New Harmony demonstrates clearly this kind of failure of the community to be able to provide a basis for unifying the individual so that they submerge their own identities.

The basic conflict between the collective and the individual values of these communities is, as already indicated, a wider phenomenon and one which occurs in all types of societies. All the locality situations that have been examined in this discussion, redevelopments, new towns, transitional communities, all have the same conflict between individual interests which are private and domestic and communal interests which vary according to the type of situation from the well articulated and explicit ideologies of the ideological communities to the much more generalised notions of the redevelopment community residents and planners.

Chapter 7

The Sociology of New Communities

I ORIGINS

The origin of new communities can be seen in a value complex, both as a reflection of the dominant values of the society where they are created as part of public policy and as a reflection of possibly emergent or alternative values in the case of the private or group creations. Common to all there seems to be a belief in the virtue of the small scale as opposed to the large-scale or mass society. This belief has provided a continuing theme of discussion regarding the nature of the residential environment from those who were initially struck by the seemingly disruptive effects of the onset of industrialisation upon activities and communities to the contemporary 'communitarians' who advocate a return to the simpler life away from environmental pollution and problems of modern technocratic society. In this social background there are a number of different strands to be identified. There is the nineteenth-century social reform tradition, which accepted the city but considered that it needed to be improved and controlled. The principal concern of the reformers was with limitations on such things as hours of work and improvements in conditions of work and living via housing, health and hygiene measures. These resulted in the twentieth century in a single pressure group channelled through the garden cities and later the town planning associations, to advocate systematic control over urban growth and the deliberate creation of new urban communities as part of that policy. Alongside this reform tradition there have been those writers and thinkers who were concerned with social reconstruction of a more fundamental type. These were mostly middle-class intellectuals who were aware of and desired to remove the faults of the industrial cities. Among their number, Owen and Fourier[1] with their utopian socialist community experiments were important in the nineteenth century as were the less ideological developments at Bournville, Saltaire and Port Sunlight. In the twentieth century Howard,[2] Le Corbusier[3] and

Frank Lloyd Wright[4] stand out from among others as proponents of different solutions for the future path of urban development. Currently the reform and social reconstruction traditions appear to have merged into a social philosophy which stresses the need to break up the city to recreate 'small communities', to reintroduce the local community via community development and neighbourhood associations. This leads to the new advocacy of social planning rather than physical or economic planning, which would emphasise social relationships within the environment and bring about more involvement and participation of the citizen in community life. The young Liberals' strategy and philosophy is, for example, expressed in these terms. Although this social philosophy is perhaps the emergent one, it is by no means the universally accepted, therefore, it is important to appreciate that alternative sets of values exist regarding the shape of new communities.

Alongside these values there have been those who have rejected contemporary society, no matter what this society was like, and have created their own versions of society through the establishment of communes. This activity is still very much a part of contemporary society with the continuing development of new communes within many countries by those who are rejecting the dominant values and modes of living in urban industrial society. This rejection is expressed in the development of alternative political systems, like the utopian socialists, or religious-based systems like the Hutterites or a kind of 'naturalism' like the 'digger' and other 'earth culture' groups who concentrate upon a return to a simpler life without modern technology and concentrate upon the use of only 'natural' materials.

II PROCESS OF NEW COMMUNITY DEVELOPMENT

The second element in the model is that of the process of development. Here it is necessary to distinguish between social allocation, the role of individuals holding key positions, voluntarism and scale of development.

(a) *Social Allocation*

The first feature in the process of community formation, that of social allocation, is the one which reflects the political and economic system in operation within a society.[5] It will, therefore, vary somewhat depending upon whether the country is, for example, democratic with a free enterprise market economy or a socialist state with a command economy.[6] Variations will arise depending on whether central or local planning is practised and whether the planning system is one of administrative or legal controls.[7] The variations which differences in political systems can bring about in the allocation of individuals to residential areas can be clearly seen in looking at Western Europe and Eastern Europe where the contrast is between democratic, market economies and socialist command economies. In Western Europe the system of allocation is primarily one of private leadership modified by regulations upon their activities imposed by national and local governments. This is in contrast to the socialist command economy where the state regulates more directly and takes initiative through public developments. In the market economies the economic base of residential segregation, through the operation of the land and housing market, has been prominent in urban theory. For example, in the Chicago School of Ecology, one of the profound influences was the Ricardian theory of rents.[8] Rents were seen as one of the initial allocators of people to sections of the city. Once these initial allocations were made the reputational character of the area was established and growth was then also the product of like attracting like, so supporting the 'ecology and natural areas' view of city growth. But at the heart of the residential segregation was basically the operation of the market forces working in a largely uncontrolled way. This kind of market allocation is still central to the distribution within contemporary British cities although they are modified by planning controls. This means that a comprehension of the allocation mechanisms requires a knowledge both of the planning modes used and the administrative rules and procedures operated by local and national governments.

Within Britain planning operates within two modes. One is adaptive which is concerned with the analysis of current problems and the development of solutions, for example, for such things as car parking, traffic management, etc. This means that the allocation of resources within the city and localities between various activities, e.g. housing, transport, roads, education, etc., is one of bargaining between various departments and between various interest groups and political parties. In this type of planning each decision is bargained over separately so that no overall strategy appears, consequently planning is basically haphazard. The second type of planning is normative. Here the future is more the concern of the planner than the immediate situation and solutions are proposed which incorporate a view of the future. This kind of planning can be of two types. The first is one which attempts to extrapolate current trends and so arrive at an idea of what the future will look like, e.g. calculate the rising number of motor cars and on this basis, plan the road and car parking programme. This type of plan may propose a modification of the trends revealed but these are likely to be adjustments rather than radical changes. The majority of the policy plans produced in recent years by local authorities in Britain are of this type. The second type is where a deliberate attempt is made to create the future by changing the existing system of allocation of resources to both individuals and groups and also probably the procedures of allocation. The need for normative planning is clearly demonstrated in a recent study by Reichhardt[9] into the problem of traffic congestion in European cities. By using games theory he shows that individuals will not voluntarily give up using their cars as they believe that such unilateral action by them would merely allow someone else to fill up the space they leave by not using their car to travel to the city. The problem, therefore, can only be solved by collective actions which involve a more positive approach by the planners and local government and consequently the likelihood of conflict of interests. For example, the extension of the road system, as was proposed in the London Motorway Box, would have destroyed areas of the city and changed its character.

The planning of activities within Britain operates within an administrative framework where the local planning officers and committees work within a framework of rules laid down in national policy, through government circulars and through legislative action. So the way in which these rules are operated affects the allocation of individuals within a locality. The same kind of situations exists with communities which are outside the public control sphere like squatter colonies and communes except that here the rules are applied and constructed by the community itself rather than by external agencies. Within the private sector there are planning controls over the siting of housing and other building, size, type and nature of construction and broader rules concerning the balance between different sorts of land use and activities within an area, demonstrated by the decision of the Department of the Environment not to approve the current Greater London Council plan for Covent Garden redevelopment. One of the important reasons here was that the plan did not preserve enough residential development. Secondly, in the private sector there are rules operated by building societies, insurance companies and other financiers. The operation of these rules favours the person with a salaried secure occupation buying new property, therefore they are selective of certain categories of the population. Thirdly, there is the role of the estate agent as one who helps to direct particular categories of 'buyers' to certain sections of the market: the young married couple with a rising secure income to the new suburban housing estates and the coloured immigrant to the declining middle-class areas of the city. Thus within this part of the housing market there is an allocative mechanism which selects certain categories for residence in particular areas and types of community.

The public sector of housing, about one-third, in Britain is similarly governed by rules of eligibility for council housing.[10] The main elements which discriminate here are residential qualifications which have to be met before the family is placed on the waiting list. Once on the list the allocation is on the basis of the 'points system' which is often weighted for length of residence. These residential qualifications tend to be strictest in the areas with the greatest housing needs. In those areas, therefore, the lists are long and movement up them is slow. Further, in such areas of housing shortage, land costs are often high and, therefore, local authority building programmes are expensive and limited. If these various conditions are met, the final placement of the family in a housing area will depend upon the means used to place families by the local authority housing department. In a recent study of an area of Glasgow, for example, the researcher[11] argues that conformity to the value precepts of the city housing department was the requirement for the attainment of good quality council housing in a suburban rather than central location.

This leads to the consideration of differential desires within the population to attain residence within particular residential settings. Here the social reputation of an area is very important. Social reputation is dependent upon the believed nature of the population and their practices as much, if not more, than upon the actual. There exist, within the urban area, a variety of residential locations possessing different social reputations, which reflect different values. These vary from 'suburban' values of the lower-middle-class new housing estates[12] to the 'delinquent low reputation' of the older central city areas. The study of the Glasgow central area showed how marked discrepancies can arise between the official view of what goes on in an area, that of the residents and the actual behaviour observed by an investigator. These social reputations are, in part, related to the class and economic position of individuals and, therefore, to the market nature of the housing allocation system.[13]

The process of community formation, therefore, in market economies with democratic political systems is one which requires the examination of the politico-economic system particularly as this emerges in the planning modes and allocation procedures. These two factors determine both the range and the type of new communities which are produced through public initiation.

In contrast to the system of Western European society, within the command economies of socialist states there are differences produced in the type and form of community because of variations in this basic process of social allocation. The absence of the market as a distributor means that income, house price and rent level are no longer vital considerations. Further, the nature of the system makes owner-occupation the most disadvantaged state rather than renting. The owner-occupier, for example, has to maintain his property which is most likely to be old and he is unable to enjoy the benefits of the subsidised newer rental accommodation. The allocation of people to housing in these systems is even more heavily tied to the planners and the administrative rules operated than in, for example, Britain. There is evidence from Hungary[14] and Czechoslovakia[15] which shows how these rules are operated and their effects upon the residential structure. Konrad and Szelenyi show for Hungary how the allocators reward differentially and systematically by giving a higher proportion of modern tenancies to those with the highest socio-economic level. This produces a similar kind of income related distribution of housing classes as is found in Western cities. In another study by Musil of Prague, it is shown that the rules have led to new property being allocated to key employees and by size and structure of the family. This has resulted in the age of property being in many cases, related to the age of the occupiers.

Clearly, therefore, a first major variable in community formation is the process of social allocation as it emerges out of the politico-economic system of the society. This system determines the modes of planning and the type of administrative controls over housing and residential development.

(b) *Role of Key Position Holders*

A second main variable in community formation is the actual individuals and groups who hold key positions, for example, the planners, the politicians, the community and neighbourhood organisations, new town commissioners, etc.

Planners, like planning, operate within a framework of differing goals. There appear to be two types of planner who can be distinguished: those who see themselves simply as individuals who solve particular problems which are presented to them, operating essentially as technical experts and, secondly, those who are committed to more positive philosophies, either in terms of improving or creating a 'good' or better physical environment or those who encompass a broad view of creating total new environments which comprise both physical and social dimensions. Because of their training and position within the decision-making procedures of local government, the planners are likely to be in a situation where role conflict is common. This is particularly the case where they are mediating between competing or conflicting interests when there may be conflict between their reference group as planners, i.e. their professional group and their reference group as local authority employees.

The second group which is important is the political group, both national and local, in the case of the 'publicly sponsored' new developments and the controlling groups of the pre-new community organisations in the case of other communities, e.g. squatters and communes. In the case of public developments, the decision to embark upon a programme of new community construction in Britain and many other countries is a political one, brought about in many cases by the persistent advocacy of a small but influential group. Similarly, at a local level, decisions about the expansion or otherwise of villages, the redevelopment of an area of the town, the siting of a new road, etc., are essentially political decisions made as a result of a bargaining process between different pressure and interest groups.

The final group who have some control over this process are the 'gate-keepers' or those responsible for the actual selection of individuals for residence in any particular area.[16] Obviously, the ease or difficulty of access will vary depending upon the nature of the community. For example, in a market economy price is crucial but there are also gates to house ownership via mortgage loans, which make the building society manager a potential gate-keeper. Also there is the estate agent who may advise or direct different categories of people to different sectors of the housing market. In the PEP report,[17] for example, on racial discrimination in Britain, it was shown that both groups discriminated against immigrants and this was one reason why they have been found predominantly in areas of transition within the centre of cities. Another group which has operated in this way is the new town housing departments who have practised a policy of housing allocation linked to jobs within the new town. This has led to discrimination in favour of skilled manual workers and younger age groups both of which are over-represented in the new towns. In the case of public sector housing there are the housing visitors and managers who have an influential position as they have the task of making recommendations regarding the nature of accommodation and area to be offered to particular families. In the socialist countries these latter groups have greater powers as the majority of housing allocation comes under their control.

In the non-publicly controlled new communities there are groups such as the *favela* associations and kibbutz councils who control the entry of individuals to their communities. For example, in one of the *barriada* associations of Lima, the allocation of plots was made almost entirely to families rather than to single persons, thus affecting the nature of the communities, both as they were formed and as they have subsequently developed.[18]

(c) *Voluntarism*

A third factor in community formation is the degree of voluntarism or choice involved. In the creation of new local authority housing estates, the new residents have little choice, either being rehoused or qualifying from the waiting list. The residents of the new suburban areas have more choice, although here this is limited by the housing market and their income level. The move to a new town is limited by the range of jobs that the individual is qualified to undertake. In transitional urban communities, the choice is limited by the availability of vacant land and the controls operated by squatter associations and governmental authorities. In the communes, choice is exercised more by the community than by the individual, i.e. the question of whether they are willing to accept him as a member.

(d) *Scale of Development*

The final variable is the scale of the development and the degree to which self-sufficiency is aimed at as a goal. This varies considerably from the 100,000 plus at one of the London County Council's housing projects to the 80–120 of the Hutterite communities to the 6–12 of some of the contemporary communes.

The model of community formations presented so far, therefore, suggests that new communities find their origin in the social value complex of a society which provides alternative values and consequently the possibility of conflict. The process of formation is characterised by social allocation, activities of key individuals and groups, voluntarism, scale and independence. Within this process there operates social conflict, both between the groups and within the process of allocation, as the allocation is concerned with the distribution of limited and valued resources. The process consequently reflects the power system in operation in society, i.e. who gets what and why. The system of allocation which is seen as a central process in determining housing and residential segregation is not only concerned with these two attributes of urban society, but also with education, social services, transport, sports and recreational facilities, in fact everything with which economic and social planning is concerned. The resultant of this process is the range of new communities that can be identified. These will now be examined in relation to the degree to which they reflect 'positive' creation.

III   TYPES OF NEW COMMUNITIES

(a)   *Partial Communities*

The first type are partial communities which are not independent but dependent upon the city which is usually the source of the majority of their population. This category would include housing estates, suburbs and commuter villages. These are the result for the most part of adaptive planning, of providing answers to specific needs at specific times, usually housing, rather than an overall plan of the future environment to be created. The decision regarding the siting of the houses, the type of layout, etc., is part of the process of conflict and constraint which surrounds decision-making where individual and collective interests come into contact, like for example, in the Covent Garden redevelopment proposals. The scheme and the government's decision illustrate the conflicts between the different interest groups involved, the property developers, the present residents, the Greater London Council and the Department of the Environment. These conflicts are resolved through a series of compromises between the conflicting interests, like for example, the decision to raise the future residential population to 3,500. Another current example is the Layfield Committee's Report on the London Motorway Box scheme.[19] Further within these new developments, the nature of the community has in many cases been affected by the conflicts which developed between the new residents and the outside authorities and neighbouring populations. For example in the saga of the Cuttesloe Walls[20] in Oxford, where a wall was erected across a road by a middle-class private estate to insulate the residents from a council estate. The subsequent removal of this wall by the local authority was the result of a protracted struggle. Conflicts, of which the Cuttesloe Walls is an extreme case, were initially responsible for giving the community cohesion and identity.

(b)   *New Towns*

The second type is the new town where the planning is moving more to a normative position of positive creation, where the community has been guided and developed according to a definite plan which incorporates many of the goals of contemporary social philosophy regarding the reduction of scale of living and the creation of smaller residential units which might develop into local systems of social relationships of a meaningful kind. The emergence of new towns and the control policies associated with them can be seen to have been through a process of conflict, e.g. conflict between those who desired city control and those who did not, political pressure and opportunism. The emergence of a new town policy elsewhere than Britain was, in some cases, prevented through a conflict of interests, e.g. in America although advocated by the federal government as part of a policy to deal with American cities, the proposals were defeated by the city governments, real estate, insurance and commercial interests.[21] Currently in New Zealand it is advocated by the government for the South Island and opposed by the majority of the existing South island local bodies who feel it will attract population and income away from their areas, and the affected land owners.

(c) *Transitional Urban Communities*

The transitional urban communities which have marked the development of Third World cities again very clearly illustrate how social conflict plays a key role in their formation. The transitional communities are an expression of the values and goals of people within the cities. Their demands are for shelter, security of tenure and community facilities. These are in direct conflict with the official housing norms of the government which give priority to housing of modern standards built via loans which defer the attainment of ownership until after the loan has been repaid. This does not give the kind of guarantees of security which the individuals define as of fundamental importance. This difference of goals means that the squatters erect and develop community facilities as a means of establishing the existence of their community much more rapidly than they complete their houses. Conflict of a different type between the community and the state, in the form of its agents, e.g. the police, is also important for establishing community identity and is an aid to the quick and effective development of the community.

(d) *Ideological Communities*

The final type is that of the ideological communities which, like the transitional, are created outside the 'public' system of planning and development by those who accept alternative values to those predominant in the society. This means that they are very often in conflict with the rest of the society in which they are situated. For example, the history of the Hutterite development in North America has been marked by conflicts between them and the local American populations, these conflicts arising out of their distinctive values, dress and behaviour.

The communities can, therefore, be seen as having emerged out of a complex social process within which conflict about goals, mediation by public and private bodies and individuals and constraints upon actions have operated to produce the particular pattern of new communities that can be observed in any particular society. This means that to understand community formation, it is necessary to explore social processes, particularly that of social conflict and constraint within the city and society. This cannot be comprehended without a consideration of the political and economic systems and power distribution within the society.

IV   COMMUNITY PERSISTENCE

From the consideration of the model of community formation it could be predicted that the stability of the communities formed would vary according to the extent to which they arose in the response to the needs of the inhabitants and the extent to which they were planned creations. In the new estates, studies showed evidence of a 'phase hypothesis'[22] whereby the degree of communal solidarity declined over time to give way to an individualistic pattern of living where external criteria of status and position became paramount. The new towns would appear to have followed a similar kind of path in that individual life styles appear to have become prominent along with class segregation, destroying the ideals of 'social balance' and community planning. The transitional communities also in many ways conform to the phase hypothesis in that, as they become more permanently based and secure in their acceptance as recognised parts of the city, so they also experience the weakening of community organisation and a lower level of participation in activities by the residents who turn increasingly to the development of their own plots and houses. The ideological communities have the longest continuous existence as distinctive communities and here the answer lies in the nature of their organisation and, more importantly, in the acceptance of their basic values by the members of the community. Where this has not been the case then internal conflict over the community has led to its short duration.

From this discussion the degree of permanence of new communities lies in a number of factors. The first is the existence of some unifying element. This can be of two types, an instrumental reason or a value. The first case would cover the relatively short-lived 'communities' of the new housing estates where there is need for common action to deal with the various authorities, builders, etc., regarding the completion of the development work and adequacy of provisions. As soon as this instrumental reason for cohesion is lost, the community quickly disintegrates. The second case is where the community has some kind of value consensus amongst both the current members, the founders and the new recruits who are ideally screened to discover the extent of their adherence to the values of the community. The Hutterites and the kibbutzim, the longest running 'new communities' both have a procedure for admittance which is not automatic even for those born into the community. In both these cases both the individual and the community make a conscious decision regarding the entry of new individuals into full community membership. These tests for entry are attempts to examine the extent to which the intending member knows and shares the values of the community. The second factor is the means employed to cope with the organisation of community life and to resolve the internal conflicts within the community and deal with the conflicts and tensions which arise between the community and society. In all the new communities there exist two kinds of conflict and constraint which are important at different times for the pattern of development. The conflict between the 'estate', new town resident, *favela* resident, commune dweller, and the rest of his society, is one kind which affects the stability and longevity of the community and the other is that between the community itself and its members. Conflicts between the society and the community lasted the shortest time on average on the new estate. These being the areas where 'communities' were the least stable, and the longest time in the ideological communities which were most stable. Conflicts between the community and society can, therefore, be seen as functional to the integration and stability of a community. The second type, between the community and the individual, is found in all the types of new communities examined and depending on the way in which it is coped with, the stability of the communities will vary. For example, within the kibbutz there are conflicts regarding the role of paid labour, the extent of private ownership permissible, the standard of living and the relationships of parent and children. These conflicts over goals and values lead to 'crises' in the kibbutz. The Hutterites also have experienced similar conflicts between individual desires and the collective values of their community. In both these cases, because of the extent to which the members share a basic set of agreed values relating to the benefits and superiority of communal living, the disagreements have been accommodated through modifications of the rules of behaviour rather than leading to disintegration as happened through failures of such procedures in the Owenite community at New Harmony.

The final ingredient in the determination of community stability is the existence of an effective system of social organisation, both economic with clear division of labour and allocation of function and through the existence of democratic decision-making procedures which give the members of the community an involvement with their own government. The organisation in a sense is simplified in the longest established new communities by their agricultural base and physical semi-isolation. These characteristics are not found in the new estate or new town where it is very largely the degree of dependence upon the city which varies.

The outlines of a model of the sociology of new communities have now been drawn. The model has its point of origin in the social values of the society. For new community development, the values which emphasise the importance of living within small-scale communities must be present. This initial idea is then subject to the process of social allocation which has as its central mechanism social conflict around the goals, means and ends of the participants, the politicians, the planners and the people, in the creation of a new community. This process creates principally four broad types of new community which, because of their nature, of their structure and development, have varying degrees of permanence within society.

V   SOCIAL PLANNING: A POSTSCRIPT

The elaboration of the process whereby new communities are created raises a number of issues which are relevant to the current arguments regarding the development of social planning and the wider involvement of the public in the process of planning. The aims of social planning appear to be the maximisation of opportunity and a widening of choice for individuals and communities, not only in housing and residential location but over the whole gamut of services and facilities provided within the city, i.e. education, health, etc.[23] The model presented here demonstrates that the current restrictions of choice within Britain lie largely in the process of social allocation by both the economic pressures of, for example, housing costs and rent levels and the operation of the rules and procedures of eligibility to different kinds of opportunities within the urban environment. The extension of choice is problematic as all systems have allocative procedures which incorporate constraints upon the free choice of individuals and communities. These patterns of constraint can be changed and will give different opportunities to individuals and groups, but greater actual freedom of choice may well not be achieved. The modification of planning procedures to make them more responsive to the planned for, will not achieve their goal unless the working of the present process of community formation, with its in-built constraints on the nature of individual choice, is appreciated.

A further problem arises, regarding the development of a social planning which both creates choice and provides safeguards for the environment. This is demonstrated most clearly by the current problem of the role of the private motorist and cars within the city. As the study cited earlier showed, car drivers were each individually unwilling to give up their motor car, whilst at the same time conceding that the number of cars entering the city should be reduced. This means that the reduction in the number of cars requires normative planning, which establishes new goals and value preferences which do not extend choice so much as restrict and redirect choice from, in this case, private to public urban transport systems. This, then, is an illustration of the basic nature of the conflict between individual and community values, which is demonstrated in all studies of new communities, whatever their reason for development. It is also an example of the somewhat contradictory aims of the recent arguments regarding the need for and nature of 'social planning' within the urban environment. There is clearly a need for the comprehension of the social dimension of planning in changing a given urban environment and in the procedures adopted to create new communities. It is, however, imperative that these be based upon a correct and careful diagnosis of the situation and the complex of social processes which are part and parcel of the urban environment. The lack of such comprehension can only perpetuate the piecemeal, adaptive methods of approach that have been used in the past in relation to the planning and design of both new and existing urban environments.

Notes and References

Chapter 1

[1] See M. and L. White, *The Intellectual Versus the City* (Mentor Books, 1964); H. Stretton, *Ideas for Australian Cities* (Georgian House, Melbourne, 1970); A. Strauss, *Images of the American City* (Free Press, 1968), Lewis Mumford, *The City in History* (Secker & Warburg, 1961); Jane Jacobs, *The Death and Life of Great American Cities* (Johnathan Cape, 1962).

[2] B. Berry and F. E. Horton, *Geographical Perspectives on Urban Systems* (Prentice Hall, 1970).

[3] W. Christaller, *Central Places in Southern Germany* (Prentice Hall, 1966).

[4] B. Berry, *Spatial Analysis* (Prentice Hall, 1968); A. Losch, *The Economics of Location*, 1954.

[5] E. W. Burgess and D. J. Bogue, *Contributions to Urban Sociology* (University of Chicago Press, 1964).

[6] G. D. Suttles, *The Social Construction of Communities* (University of Chicago Press, 1972).

[7] F. Tönnies, *Community and Society* (Harper Torchbooks, 1957). See also C. Bell and H. Newby, *Community Studies* (Allen & Unwin, 1971).

[8] Scott Greer, *The Emerging City* (Free Press, 1962).

[9] See for example: Marc Fried, 'Functions of the Working Class Community in Modern Urban Society', *Journal of the American Institute of Planners* 33, 2 (1967).

[10] D. C. Thorns, *Control of the City* (David & Charles, 1975).

Chapter 2

[1] United Nations, *A Concise Summary of the World Population Situation in 1970* (UN, 1971), pp. 25–7.

[2] K. Davis, *World Urbanisation 1950–1970*, Vol. I, Basic Data for Cities, Countries and Regions, Population Monograph Series No. 4, 1969; vol II, Analysis of Trends, Relationships and Developments, No. 9, 1972 (California Institute of International Studies, California University Press).

[3] United Nations, *A Concise Summary of World Population*, op. cit., p. 28.

[4] J. B. Cullingworth, *Problems of an Urban Society* (Allen & Unwin, 1972), vol. I, ch. 1.

[5] L. Wirth, 'Urbanism as a Way of Life', in A. J. Reiss (ed.), *On Cities and Social Life* (University of Chicago Press, 1964).

[6] E. W. Burgess, 'The Growth of the City', in R. E. Park, E. W. Burgess and R. D. McKenzie (eds.), *The City* (University of Chicago Press, 1925).

[7] K. Davis, 'The Urbanisation of the Human Population', in G. Breese (ed.), *The City In Newly Developing Countries* (Prentice Hall, 1969).

[8] See for example: D. C. Thorns, *Suburbia* (MacGibbon & Kee, 1972), ch. 3.

[9] A. F. Weber, *The Growth of Cities in the Nineteenth Century* (Cornell University Press, 1963), p. 42.

[10] P. Hall, *World Cities* (World University Library, 1966), ch. 8, p. 217.

[11] Lloyd Rodwin, *Nations and Cities* (Houghton, Mifflin & Co., 1970).

[12] B. F. Hoselitz, 'A Survey of Literature on Urbanisation in India', in R. Turner (ed.), *India's Urban Future* (University of California Press, 1962); 'The Role of

Urbanisation in Economic Development—Some International Comparisons', in R. Turner (ed.), *India's Urban Future*, op. cit.; N. V. Sovani, *Urbanisation and Urban India* (Asia Publishing House, 1966).

[13] P. C. Lloyd, *Classes, Crises and Coups* (MacGibbon & Kee, 1971); F. Bailey, *Caste and the Econimic Frontier* (M.U.P., 1957).

[14] T. G. McGee, *The South-East Asian City* (C. Bell & Sons Ltd., 1967); P. Hauser, *Urbanisation in Asia and the Far East* (UNESCO, 1956).

[15] M. Juppenlatz, *Cities in Transformation: The Urban Squatter Problem of the Developing World* (University of Queensland Press, 1970).

[16] See for example: P. Hauser, *Urbanisation in Latin America* (UNESCO, 1961); R. Morse, 'Urbanisation in Latin America', *Latin American Research Review*, vol. I, no. 1 (1965); Glenn H. Beyer (ed.), *The Urban Explosion in Latin America* (Cornell University Press, 1967); Frances Violich, *Cities in Latin America* (Reinhold Publishing Corporation, 1944); F. F. Rabinovitz and F. M. Trueblood, *Latin American Urban Research* (Sage Publications, 1971).

[17] B. F. Hoselitz, *The Role of Urbanisation in Economic Development*, op. cit.

[18] Oscar Lewis, *The Children of Sanchez* (Secker & Warburg, 1962); *La Vida* (Random House, 1966).

[19] Glenn H. Beyer, *The Urban Explosion in Latin America*, op. cit., p. 101.

[20] S. D. Chapman (ed.), *The History of Working Class Housing* (David & Charles, 1971).

[21] J. B. Cullingworth, *Town and Country Planning* (Allen & Unwin, 1964), chs 1 and 10; W. Ashworth, *The Genesis of Modern Town Planning* (Routledge & Kegan Paul, 1954); L. Benvelo, *The Origins of Modern Town Planning* (Routledge & Kegan Paul, 1967).

[22] P. Abercrombie and J. H. Forshaw, *County of London Plan* (Macmillan, 1943).

[23] Ministry of Housing and Local Government, *Planning and Transport: The Leeds Approach*, 1969; J. M. Thomson, *Transport* (David & Charles, 1975); C. Buchanan, *Traffic in Towns* (Penguin, 1963).

[24] Local Government Board, *Report of the Committee on Building Construction in Connection with the Provision of Dwellings for the Working Classes* (HMSO, 1918).

[25] L. W. Creese (ed.), *The Legacy of Raymond Unwin: A Human Pattern for Planning* (M.I.T. Press, 1967).

[26] The Greater London Development Plan, Report of the Panel of Enquiry (Layfield), 1973; J. Hillman (ed.), *Planning for London* (Penguin, 1973).

[27] E. Howard, *Garden Cities of Tomorrow* (1965, reprint with preface by Sir Frederic Osborn and Introductory essay by Lewis Mumford), Faber & Faber (1965).

[28] Le Corbusier, *The City of Tomorrow and its Planning* (The Architectural Press, 1947).

[29] F. L. Wright, *The Living City* (Horizon Press, 1958).

[30] See M. and L. White, *The Intellectual Versus the City* (Mentor Books, 1964).

[31] Lewis Mumford, *The City in History*, op. cit.; Jane Jacobs, *The Death and Life of Great American Cities*, op. cit.; Scott Donaldson, *The Suburban Myth* (Columbia University Press, 1969).

[32] J. Kramer, *North American Suburbs* (The Glendessary Press, 1972).

[33] R. A. B. Leaper, *Community Work* (National Council of Social Service, 1970).

[34] City and County of the City of Exeter, 'A Corporate Plan', 1973.

[35] M. Broady, 'The Social Context of Urban Planning', *Urban Affairs Quarterly*, vol. 4, no. 3 (1969).

[36] G. E. Cherry, *Town Planning in its Social Context* (Leonard Hill, 1970).

[37] Ibid., p. 53.

[38] Report of the Committee on Public Participation in Planning, *People and Planning* (HMSO, 1969).

152   The Quest for Community

[39] D. C. Thorns, 'Participation in Rural Planning', *International Review of Community Development*, vol. 23/24 (1970).

[40] Royal Commission on the Distribution of Industrial Population (Barlow Report), Cmnd. 6513 (1940).

[41] Ministry of Town and Country Planning, Final Report of the New Towns Committee, Cmnd. 6876 (1946).

[42] P. Self, 'Town Planning in the United States and Britain', *Town Planning Review*, vol. 25.

[43] Mel Scott, *American City Planning Since 1890* (University of California Press, 1969).

[44] C. S. Stein, *Towards New Towns for America* (University of Liverpool Press, 1951).

[45] H. J. Gans, *People and Plans—Essays on Urban Problems and Solutions* (abridged edition) (Penguin, 1972); W. I. Goodman, 'The New Look in American Planning', *Journal of the American Institute of Planners*, vol. 34 (1968).

[46] M. Rein, 'Social Planning: The Search for Legitimacy', *Journal of the American Institute of Planners*, vol. 35 (1969).

[47] H. J. Gans, 'Planning for People, not Buildings', *Environment and Planning*, vol. 1 (1969).

[48] D. L. Foley, 'British Town Planning: One Ideology or Three', *British Journal of Sociology*, vol. 11, no. 3 (1960); Ruth Glass, 'The Evaluation of Planning: Some Social Considerations', *International Social Science Journal*, vol. 11 (1959).

[49] P. Davidoff, 'Advocacy and Pluralism in Planning', *Journal of the American Institute of Planners*, vol. 28 (1965).

[50] See H. J. Gans, *People and Plans*, op. cit.; R. Goodman, *After the Planners* (Penguin, 1972).

[51] A. Dunham, 'Poverty, City Planning and Liberty', in M. Stewart (ed.), *The City* (Penguin, 1972).

Chapter 3

[1] D. C. Thorns, *Suburbia*, op. cit., ch. 3, pp. 38–49.

[2] P. Willmott, *The Evolution of the Community* (Routledge & Kegan Paul, 1963).

[3] Summary of this material can be found in: J. Klein, *Samples from English Culture* (Routledge & Kegan Paul, 1965), vol. 1; R. N. Morris and J. Mogey, *The Sociology of Housing* (Routledge & Kegan Paul, 1965); R. Frankenburg, *Communities in Britain* (Penguin, 1965).

[4] T. Lupton and G. D. Mitchell, *Neighbourhood and Community* (Liverpool University Press, 1954).

[5] John Mogey, *Family and Neighbourhood* (Oxford University Press, 1956).

[6] M. Young and P. Willmott, *Family and Kinship in East London* (Penguin, 1958).

[7] N. Dennis, 'The Popularity of the Neighbourhood Idea', in R. E. Pahl (ed.), *Readings in Urban Sociology* (Pergamon, 1969).

[8] Ruth Durant, *Watling: A Survey of Social Life On A New Housing Estate* (P. S. King, 1959).

[9] R. N. Morris and J. Mogey, *The Sociology of Housing*, op. cit.

[10] J. Bellusch and M. Hausknecht, *Urban Renewal—People, Politics and Planning*.

[11] S. Greer and D. W. Minar, 'The Political Side of Urban Development and Redevelopment', in J. Bellusch and M. Hausknecht, *Urban Renewal*, op. cit. (p. 160); see also S. Greer, *The Urbane View* (Oxford University Press, 1972); J. Q. Wilson, *Urban Renewal: The Record and the Controversy* (M.I.T. Press, 1966).

[12] Bureau of U.S. Census, Survey of Families Recently Displaced From Urban Renewal Sites (March, 1965).

[13] H. J. Gans, *The Urban Villagers* (Free Press, 1965).

[14] B. Berry and F. E. Horton, *Geographical Perspectives on Urban Systems*, op. cit.

[15] I. Szelenyi, *Housing System and Social Structure*, Sociological Review Monograph, no. 17 (1972); C. Konrad and I. Szelenyi, 'Sociological Aspects of the Allocation of Housing', in *Industrialisation, Urbanisation and Ways of Life* (Institute of Sociology, Hungarian Academy of Sciences, 1971).

[16] J. Musil, 'Sociology of Urban Redevelopment Areas', *International Review of Community Development* (1966), vols. 15–16, pp. 213–37; 'The Development of Prague's Ecological Structure', in R. E. Pahl (ed.), *Readings in Urban Sociology* (Pergamon Press, 1968).

[17] P. Jephcott, *Homes in High Flats*, University of Glasgow Social and Econ. Studies, Occ. paper, No. 13 (Oliver & Boyd, 1971).

[18] Ministry of Housing and Physical Planning, *Some Data on House Building in the Netherlands* (1968), *Residential Environments* (1969).

[19] R. E. Mitchell, 'Some Implications of High Density Housing', *American Sociological Review*, vol. 36 (1971).

[20] A. Stevenson, E. Martin and J. O'Neill, *High Living* (Melbourne University Press, 1967).

[21] P. Jephcott, op. cit., p. 126.

[22] J. and R. Darke, *Health and Environment: High Flats* (Centre for Environmental Studies, University Working Paper 10, 1970).

[23] E. Gittus, *High Living and the Under 5's* (unpublished study).

[24] See also P. Jephcott and Stevenson, *et al.*, *Homes in High Flats*, op. cit.; *High Living*, op. cit.

[25] E. Wood, 'Housing Design: A Social Theory', in G. Bell and J. Tyrwhitt, *Human Identity in the Urban Environment* (Penguin, 1972).

[26] For example see P. Jephcott, *Homes in High Flats*, op. cit.; Ministry of Housing and Physical Planning (The Netherlands), *Should we build and live in houses or flats?* (1965).

[27] J. Marmor, 'Mental Health and Overpopulation', in S. T. Reid and D. L. Lyon (eds.), *Population Crisis: An Interdisciplinary Perspective* (Scott Foresman, 1972).

[28] R. E. Mitchell, *Some Implications of High Density Living*, op. cit., p. 27.

[29] S. Webb and J. Collette, *Urban Density, Crowding and Stress Reactions*, Paper presented to the Sociological Association of New Zealand (Wellington, 1973).

[30] T. Sharp, *Town and Townscape* (1968).

[31] P. Merlin, *New Towns* (Methuen, 1971), ch. 4, New Town Policy in France.

[32] P. Clerc, *et al.*, *Grandes Ensembles, Banlieues Nouvelles*, Centre de recherche d'urbanisme, Institute National d'Etude Demographiques (Presses Universitaires de France, 1967).

[33] Le Corbusier, *The City of Tomorrow and its Planning*, op. cit.

[34] See for example: Scott Donaldson, *The Suburban Myth*, op. cit.; W. M. Dobriner, *The Suburban Community* (G. P. Putnam & Sons, 1958); *Class in Suburbia* (Prentice Hall, 1963); D. C. Thorns, 'Suburban Myths and Realities', *International Review of Community Development* (1974); B. Berger, *Working Class Suburb* (University of California Press, 1968); 'The Myth of Suburbia', *Journal of Social Issues* (17/1/1961); S. D. Clark, *The Suburban Community* (University of Toronto Press, 1964).

[35] T. Ziell, 'Social Change in Levittown', in W. M. Dobriner (ed.), *Class in Suburbia*, op. cit.

[36] D. C. Thorns, 'Suburban Values and the Urban System', *International Journal of Comparative Sociology* (1975).

[37] H. J. Gans, *The Levittowners* (Allen Lane and Penguin, 1967).

[38] See for example: J. R. Seeley, R. A. Sim and E. W. Loosley, *Crestwood Heights* (Basic Books, 1956); Hannah Gavron, *The Captive Wife* (Penguin, 1970).

[39] For a review of these areas see: D. C. Thorns, *Suburbia*, op. cit., chs. 6–8; J. Kramer (ed.), *North American Suburbs*, op. cit.

[40] W. M. Dobriner, *Class in Suburbia*, op. cit., ch. 5.

[41] Ibid., p. 130.

[42] B. Berry and F. E. Horton, *Geographical Perspectives on Urban Systems*, op. cit.

[43] D. C. Thorns, *Suburbia*, op. cit., p. 54.

[44] C. Moindrot, 'The Movement of Population in the Birmingham Region', in C. Jansen (ed.), *Readings in the Sociology of Migration* (Pergamon, 1970).

[45] D. C. Thorns, *Suburbia*, op. cit., p. 56.

[46] E. Craven, 'Private Residential Expansion in Kent' and R. E. Pahl and E. Craven, 'Residential Expansion—The Role of the Private Developer in the South East' in R. E. Pahl, *Whose City?* (Longmans, 1970).

[47] C. Bell, *Middle Class Families* (Routledge & Kegan Paul, 1968).

[48] See studies by: W. M. Dobriner, 'The Natural History of a Reluctant Suburb', in W. M. Dobriner (ed.), *Class in Suburbia*, op. cit.; R. Crichton, *Commuter's Village* (David and Charles, 1964); N. Elias and J. T. Scotson, *The Established and the Outsider*, R. E. Pahl, 'Urbs in Rure', Geographical Paper no. 2 (London School of Economics and Political Science, 1965); D. C. Thorns, 'The Changing Pattern of Rural Social Stratification', *Sociologia Ruralis*, vol. viii, no. 2 (1968); V. Pons, *Social Structure of a Hertfordshire Parish*, Ph.D. thesis (University of London, 1955).

[49] L. Carey and Roy Mapes, *The Sociology of Planning* (Batsford, 1972).

[50] See also T. Caplow, *The Urban Ambience* (Bedminster Press, 1964).

[51] H. J. Gans, *The Urban Villagers*, op. cit.

[52] Oscar Lewis, *La Vida*, op. cit.

[53] M. Young and P. Willmott, *Family and Kinship in East London*, op. cit.

[54] L. Kuper (ed.), *Living in Towns* (Cresset Press, 1953).

[55] W. Watson, 'Social Mobility and Social Class In Industrial Communities', in M. Gluckman (ed.), *Closed Systems and Open Minds* (Oliver & Boyd, 1964); S. Edgell, 'Spiralists: Their Careers and Family Lives', *British Journal of Sociology* (1970).

Chapter 4

[1] E. Howard, *Garden Cities of Tomorrow*, op. cit.

[2] C. Kingsley, *Great Cities: Their Influence for Good and Evil* (1857).

[3] See Chapter 2 together with W. Peterson, *The Ideological Origins of British New Towns* (American Institute of Planners, 1968).

[4] C. B. Purdom, *The Letchworth Achievement* (Dent, 1963).

[5] For documentation on the origins of the new towns and the framework of new town legislation see: F. J. Osborn and A. Whittick, *The New Towns* (Leonard Hill, 1969), 2nd edition; F. Schaffer, *The New Town Story* (MacGibbon & Kee, 1970); Lloyd Rodwin, *The British New Town Policy* (Harvard University Press, 1956).

[6] See for example: L. Mumford, *The City in History*, op. cit.; *The Urban Prospect* (Secker & Warburg, 1968).

[7] C. S. Stein, *Toward New Towns for America* (University of Liverpool Press, 1951).

[8] T. Veblen, *The Theory of the Leisure Class* (Mentor books, 1953).

[9] C. Cooley, *Sociological Theory and Social Research—Selected Papers*, Introduction by R. C. Angell (Kelley, 1969).

[10] C. Perry, *The Neighbourhood Unit* (1929).

[11] W. L. Crease (ed.), *The Legacy of Raymond Unwin*, op. cit.

[12] D. L. Foley, 'Idea and Influence—The Town and Country Planning Association', *Journal of the American Institute of Planners*, vol. XXVIII (1962).

[13] Le Corbusier, *The City of Tomorrow*, op. cit.
[14] F. J. Osborn and A. Whittick, *The New Towns*, op. cit., p. 82.
[15] Royal Commission on the Distribution of Industrial Population, op. cit.
[16] Final Report of the New Towns Committee, op. cit.
[17] See F. Schaffer, *The New Town Story*, op. cit.
[18] A. K. Constandse, L. Wijers and N. C. de Ruiter, *Planning and Creation of an Environment* (Royal Institute of Netherlands Architects, 1963).
[19] *The Development of the Western Netherlands* (The Hague, 1958).
[20] *Rijkedienst Voor de ijsselmeer polders* (Second World Congress for Rural Sociology, 1968).
[21] A. Rogers, 'Changing Land Use in the Dutch Polders', *Journal of the Town Planning Institute* (1971).
[22] Aycliffe Expansion, Master Plan Report for the Expansion of Newton Aycliffe to a population of 45,000 (Aycliffe Development Corporation, 1967); see also Ray Thomas, *Aycliffe to Cumbernauld* (PEP Broadsheet 516, 1969).
[23] Livingston Development Plan, Livingston Development Corporation (1971).
[24] J. Thompson, 'Irvin New Town Plan', *The Architects Journal* (September 1971).
[25] Plan for Milton Keynes Volumes I and II, (Milton Keynes Development Corporation, 1970).
[26] V. A. Karn, *Aycliffe Housing Survey*, University of Birmingham Centre for Urban and Regional Studies, Occ. Paper 9 (1970).
[27] V. A. Karn, *Crawley 'Housing Survey*, University of Birmingham Centre for Urban and Regional Studies, Occ. paper 11 (1970).
[28] V. A. Karn, *Stevenage Housing Survey*, University of Birmingham Centre for Urban and Regional Studies, Occ. Paper 10 (1970).
[29] V. A. Karn, *East Kilbride Housing Survey*, University of Birmingham Centre for Urban and Regional Studies, Occ. Paper 8 (1970).
[30] Population and Social Survey 1970, Skelmersdale Development Corporation (October 1970).
[31] Home Interview Social Survey 1966, Runcorn Development Corporation (1966); The First 500 families, Social Survey, Runcorn Development Corporation (1969).
[32] A. A. Ogilvy, 'The Self-contained New Town', *Town Planning Review*, Vol. 39, no. 1 (1968).
[33] Ray Thomas, *London's New Towns: A Study of Self-contained and balanced communities*, PEP Broadsheet 510, vol. XXXV (London, 1969).
[34] M. Willis, 'Social Aspects of Urban Structure', *Town Planning Review* 1968.
[35] Plan for Milton Keynes, vol. II, op. cit., p. 27–9.
[36] T. Lee, 'Urban Neighbourhood as a Socio-Spatial Scheme', *Human Relations*, vol. 21 (1968).
[37] B. J. Heraud, 'Social Class and the New Towns', *Urban Studies*, vol. 5, no. 1 (1968).
[38] Population and Social Survey, Skelmersdale, op. cit., p. 37, Tables 26 and 27.
[39] The First 500 families, op. cit., pp. 10–11.
[40] H. Orlans, *Stevenage* (Routledge & Kegan Paul, 1952).
[41] C. Alexander, 'A City Is Not a Tree', *Design* (February 1966).
[42] Report on an Interregional Seminar on New Towns, held in London 1973 (UN, 1974).
[43] P. Merlin, *New Towns*, op. cit., ch. VI; Masao Yamada, 'Approach to the 21st Century: A Development Plan for Tokyo Metropolitan Area', in C. Bell and J. Tyrwhitt (eds.), *Human Identity in the Urban Environment*, op. cit.. R. L. Meier and I. Hoshino, 'Cultural Growth and Urban Development: Inner Tokyo 1951–68', in G. Bell & J. Tyrwhitt (eds.), op. cit. L. Bryson, *An Australian New Town* (Penguin, 1972).

156   The Quest for Community

[44] F. Gutheim, 'Europe Offers New Town Builders Experience', International City Managers Association (November 1966).
[45] Masao Yamada, *Approach to the 21st Century*, op. cit.
[46] H. von Hertzen and P. D. Spreiregen, *Building a New Town—Tapiola* (M.I.T. Press, 1971).
[47] P. Merlin, *New Towns*, op. cit., ch. IV.
[48] M. Yamada, *Approach to the 21st Century*, op. cit.; and R. Kakumuoto, 'A Case for Satellite Cities of 300,000 In Japan', in Bell and Tyrwhitt, op. cit.
[49] North-East Illinois Planning Commission, Plan Study Methodology.
[50] See P. Merlin, *New Towns*, op. cit.; C. Rapkin, 'New Towns for America: From Picture to Progress', *Journal of Finance*, no. 22 (1967); W. Alonso, 'What are New Towns For?', *Urban Studies*, no. 1 (1970).

Chapter 5

[1] United Nations General Assembly, *Housing, Building and Planning*, Report of the Secretary-General (1970).
[2] M. Juppenlatz, *Cities in Transformation*, op. cit., p. 17.
[3] C. Abrams, *Housing in the Modern World* (Faber & Faber, 1964), p. 21.
[4] J. C. Turner, 'Barriers and Channels for Housing Development in Modernising Countries', in W. Mangin (ed.), *Peasants in Cities* (Houghton Mifflin Company, 1970).
[5] Oscar Lewis, *The Children of Sanchez* (Random House, 1961); *La Vida* (Random House, 1966).
[6] A. M. MacEwen, 'Stability and Change in a Shanty Town: A Summary of Some Research Findings', *Sociology*, no. 1 (1972), pp. 41–58.
[7] J. C. Turner, in *Peasants in Cities*, op. cit.; 'Uncontrolled urban settlements: Problems and policies', *International Social Development Review*, no. 1, pp. 107–30; *Urbanisation Development Policies and Planning* (United Nations, 1968).
[8] W. Mangin, 'Similarities and Differences Between Two Types of Peruvian Communities', in W. Mangin (ed.), *Peasants in Cities*, op. cit.
[9] H. Camios, J. Turner and J. Steffian, *Urban Dwelling Environments—An Elementary Study of Settlements for the Study of Design Determinants*, M.I.T. Report No. 16 (M.I.T. Press, 1969).
[10] J. Mates Mar, 'Migration and Urbanisation: The Barriadas of Lima', in P. Hauser (ed.), *Urbanisation in Latin America* (UNESCO, Paris 1961).
[11] A. Pearse, 'Some Characteristics of Urbanisation in the City of Rio de Janeiro', in P. Hauser (ed.), *Urbanisation in Latin America* (UNESCO, Paris 1961), op. cit.
[12] F. Bonilla, 'Rio's Favelas: The Rural Slum within the city', in W. Mangin (ed.), *Peasants in Cities*, op. cit.
[13] M. Juppenlatz, *Cities in Transformation*, op. cit., p. 66.
[14] F. Bonilla 'Rio's Favelas', op. cit., pp. 78–83.
[15] Carolina Maria de Jesus, *Child of the Dark*, translated from Portuguese by St. Clair Drake (Signet Books, 1962).
[16] T. G. McGee, *The South-East Asian City*, op. cit.
[17] Special Committee Report, Office of the President, Manila, Phillipines, 'Squatting and Slum Dwelling in Metropolitan Manila', *Phillipine Sociological Review* (1968), vol. 16, p. 94.
[18] M. Juppenlatz, *Cities in Transformation*, op. cit., p. 114.
[19] See T. G. McGee, *The South-East Asian City*, op. cit.; G. Breese, *Urbanisation in Newly Developing Countries* (Prentice Hall, 1966), pp. 67–8; Quazi Ahmed, *Indian Cities* (University of Chicago Press, 1965).
[20] J. Abu-Lughod, *Cairo: 1001 Years of the City Victorious* (Princeton University Press, 1971).
[21] J. Abu-Lughod, Ibid., pp. 193–201.

[22] A. R. Romanis, 'Illegal Settlements in Athens', in P. Oliver, *Shelter and Society* (Cresset Press, 1969).

[23] J. Abu-Lughod, *Cairo*, op. cit., p. 129.

[24] United Nations, *Report of the Interregional Seminar on Slums and Uncontrolled Settlements—Medelin Columbia* (UN, 1971).

[25] Department of Economic and Social Affairs, *Proposals for Action on Finance for Housing, Building and Planning* (UN, 1972).

[26] United Nations, *Report of the Ad Hoc Group of Experts on Housing and Urban Development* (UN, 1962).

[27] United Nations, *Report of the U.N. Seminar on Financing of Housing and Related Community Facilities for the Arab States—Cairo, Egypt* (UN, 1963).

[28] O. H. Koenigsberger, 'The Ghana Roof Loan Scheme', prepared for the meeting on Technical and Social Problems of Urbanisation with emphasis on financing of Housing—Addis Ababa (UN, 1969); Department of Economic and Social Affairs, *Housing in Africa* (UN, 1965); P. Marris, *Family and Social Change in an African City* (Routledge & Kegan Paul, 1961); R. Weitz, *Urbanisation and the Developing Countries* (Praeger, 1973).

[29] J. C. Turner, *Uncontrolled Urban Settlements: Problems and Policies*, op. cit.

[30] Franz Fanon, *The Wretched of the Earth*, translated from the French by C. Farrington (MacGibbon & Kee, 1965), p. 103.

[31] Oscar Lewis, 'The Culture of Poverty', *Scientific American*, vol. 215, no. 4 (1966), p. 23.

[32] M. Weiner, 'Urbanisation and Political Protest', *Civilisations*, XVII (1967).

[33] G. Soares and R. L. Hamblin, 'Socio-Economic Variables and Voting for the Radical Left in Chile—1952', *American Political Science Review*, LXI (1967).

[34] W. Mangin, *Latin American Squatter Settlements*, op. cit.

[35] J. C. Turner and R. Fichter (eds.), *Freedom to Build* (Collier Macmillan, 1973).

[36] P. C. Lloyd, *Classes, Crises and Coups*, op. cit.; K. Little, *West African Urbanisation*, op. cit.; Quazi Ahmed, *Indian Cities*, op. cit.

[37] L. R. Beattie, *View from the Barrio* (University of Michigan Press, 1965).

[38] J. Abu-Lughod, *Cairo*, op. cit., p. 196.

[39] J. Lelyveld, 'Kishan Babu', in W. Mangin (ed.), *Peasants in Cities*, op. cit.; G. Breese, *Urbanisation in Newly Developing Countries*, op. cit., pp. 65–8.

[40] M. Juppenlatz, *Cities in Transformation*, op. cit., p. 66.

Chapter 6

[1] H. Darin-Drabkin, *The Other Society* (Victor Gollancz, 1962), pp. 1–53.

[2] The two main studies of the Hutterite communities are: J. W. Bennett, *Hutterian Brethren: The Agricultural Economy and Social Organisation of a Communal People* (Stanford University Press, 1967); and J. A. Hostetler and G. E. Huntingdon, *The Hutterites in North America* (Holt, Rinehart & Winston, 1967), Case Studies in Cultural Anthropology.

[3] J. W. Bennett, *Hutterian Brethren*, op. cit., pp. 143–60.

[4] J. W. Bennett, 'The Communal Brethren of the Great Plains', *Trans-action* (1966), vol. 4, pt. 2, p. 43.

[5] R. C. Cook, 'The North American Hutterites: A Study in Human Multiplication', *Population Bulletin*, no. 10 (UN, 1954).

[6] J. A. Hostetler and G. E. Huntingdon, *The Hutterites in North America*, op. cit., pp. 21–3.

[7] C. Bertha Clark, 'The Hutterian Communities—Parts I and II', *Journal of Political Economy* (1924).

[8] J. W. Eaton, 'Controlled Acculturation: A Survival Technique of the Hutterites', *American Sociological Review* (1952), vol. 17, no. 3, pp. 331–40.

[9] J. W. Bennett, *The Hutterian Brethren*, op. cit., p. 53.

[10] For a look at the development of communal societies in North America see: C. Nordhoff, *The Communist Societies of North America* (Hillary House Publishers, 1961 reprint), first published 1875.

[11] Mark Holloway, *Heavens on Earth: Utopian Communities in America 1680–1880* (Turnstile Press, 1951), pp. 101–18.

[12] A. E. Bestor, *Backwood Utopias: The Sectarian and Owenite Phases of Communitarian Socialism in America 1663–1829* (Oxford University Press, 1950).

[13] A. E. Bestor, Ibid., p. 188.

[14] M. Spiro, *Kibbutz: Venture in Utopia* (Schocken Books, 1967), ch. 2.

[15] Dan Leon, *The Kibbutz: A New Way of Life* (Pergamon Press, 1969), section II.

[16] M. Spiro, *Children of the Kibbutz* (Harvard University Press, 1958).

[17] H. Darin-Drabkin and H. Linden-Nadler, 'The Patterns of Democratic Management and Economic Efficiency in the Kibbutz', *Sociologia Ruralis*, vol. XII (1972).

[18] H. Darin-Drabkin, *The Other Society* op. cit., part III 'The Social Test'.

[19] G. Friedman, *The End of the Jewish People* (Hutchinson, 1967), pp. 62–70.

[20] A. Viteles, *A History of the Cooperative Movement in Israel*, Book II The Evolution of the Kibbutz (Vallentine-Mitchell, 1967), p. 329 et seq.

[21] Dan Leon, *The Kibbutz*, op. cit., p. 161.

[22] H. Darin-Drabkin, *The Other Society*, op. cit., p. 205; and G. Friedman, *The End of the Jewish People*, op. cit., pp. 42–7.

[23] Dan Leon, *The Kibbutz*, op. cit., p. 188.

[24] H. Darin-Drabkin, *The Other Society*, op. cit., p. 319.

[25] Clem Gorman, *Making Communes*, Survey/Manual (Whole Earth Tools, 1971), p. 8.

[26] A. Rigby, 'Communes and Social Change in Britain', *Journal of the Commune Movement*, no. 37 (March 1971); *Alternative Realities* (Routledge & Kegan Paul, 1970).

[27] Clem Gorman, *Making Communes*, op. cit., p. 14.

[28] Figure is for the number of journals printed in December 1972. This number has fallen from 3,000 in 1971.

[29] G. Davies, *The Early Stuarts—1603–1660*, Oxford History of England (Oxford University Press, 1959), p. 171.

[30] W. Laxton, *A Study of some recently formed Christian Communities in England*, unpublished MA dissertation (University of Bristol, 1972).

[31] *Directory of Communes 1970* (Communes Movement, London).

[32] *Directory of Communes 1972* (Communes Movement, London).

[33] W. Laxton, *A Study of some recently formed Christian Communities in England*, op. cit., p. 93.

[34] H. F. Infield, *Utopia and Experiment: Essays in the Sociology of Cooperation* (Atlantic Press, 1956), p.186.

Chapter 7

[1] Mark Holloway, *Heavens on Earth: Utopian Communities in America—1680–1880*, op. cit.

[2] E. Howard, *Garden Cities of Tomorrow*, op. cit.

[3] Le Corbusier, *The City of Tomorrow*, op. cit.

[4] F. L. Wright, *The Living City*, op. cit.

[5] R. E. Pahl, 'Spatial Structure and Social Structure', from *Whose City* by R. E. Pahl, op. cit.

[6] J. Fisher, 'Planning the City of Socialist Man', *Journal of American Institute of Planners*, vol. 34 (1963).

[7] P. Self, *Town Planning in the United States and Britain*, op. cit.

[8] R. E. Park, E. W. Burgess and R. D. McKenzie (eds.), *The City* (University of

Chicago Press, 1925).

[9] R. Reichhardt, 'New Behaviour Patterns and Life Styles in the Modern City', *Grosstadt Probleme*, II (Europahans, Wein, 1968).

[10] See J. Rex, 'The Sociology of the Zone of Transition', in R. E. Pahl (ed.), *Readings in Urban Sociology*, op. cit.; 'The Concept of Housing Class and the Sociology of Race Relations', *Race* 12 (3), pp. 293–301.

[11] Sean Damar, *Wine Alley: The Sociology of a Reputation*, paper presented to the BSA—Sociology Teachers Section Conference, Leeds (1972); see also: J. B. Cullingworth, *Problems of an Urban Society*, op. cit., vol. 2, pp. 49–55.

[12] D. C. Thorns, *Suburbia*, op. cit.

[13] Also of value here is G. D. Suttles, *The Social Construction of Communities*, op. cit.

[14] G. Konrad and I. Szelenyi, 'Sociological Aspects of the Allocation of Housing', op. cit.

[15] J. Musil, *The Development of Prague's Ecological Structure*, op. cit.

[16] Roy Haddon, 'A Minority in a Welfare State Society: The Location of West Indians in the London Housing Market', *The New Atlantis*, vol. 2, no. 1 (1970).

[17] W. Daniels, *Racial Discrimination in Britain* (Penguin Books, 1968).

[18] W. Mangin, 'Similarities and Differences Between Two Types of Peruvian Communities', op. cit.

[19] Greater London Development Plan, Report of the Panel of Enquiry (1973), op. cit.; also D. C. Thorns, *Control of the City*, op. cit.

[20] P. Collison, *The Cuttesloe Walls* (Faber & Faber, 1963).

[21] Mel Scott, *American City Planning*, op. cit.

[22] R. Morris and J. Mogey, *The Sociology of Housing*, op. cit.

[23] See G. Cherry, *Town Planning in its Social Context* op. cit.

Index